Information Law

Compliance for librarians, information
professionals and knowledge managers

Every purchase of a Facet book helps to fund CILIP's advocacy, awareness and accreditation programmes for information professionals.

Information Law

Compliance for librarians, information professionals and knowledge managers

Charles Oppenheim
Adrienne Muir
Naomi Korn

facet
publishing

Published by Facet Publishing,
7 Ridgmount Street, London WC1E 7AE
www.facetpublishing.co.uk

Facet Publishing is wholly owned by CILIP: the Library and Information Association.

British Library Cataloguing in Publication Data
A catalogue record for this book is available from the British Library.

ISBN 978–1–78330–366–3 (paperback)
ISBN 978–1–78330–367–0 (hardback)
ISBN 978–1–78330–368–7 (e-book)

First published 2020

Text printed on FSC accredited material.

Typeset from authors' files in 10/14 pt Linotype Palatino and Myriad Pro by Flagholme Publishing Services.
Printed and made in Great Britain by CPI Group (UK) Ltd, Croydon, CR0 4YY.

Contents

List of acronyms

ARROW   Accessible Registries of Rights Information and Orphan Works
AUP   acceptable use policy
CC   Creative Commons
CLA   Copyright Licensing Agency
DACS   Design and Artists Copyright Society
DAM   digital asset management system
DPIA   data protection impact assessment
DPO   data protection officer
EC   European Commission
ECJ   European Court of Justice
EDPB   European Data Protection Board
EEA   European Economic Area
EU   European Union
ERA   Educational Recording Agency
FOB   Firms Out of Business database
FoI   freedom of information
GDPR   General Data Protection Regulation
HEI   higher education institution
IAR   information asset register
ICO   Information Commissioner's Office
IP   intellectual property
IPR   intellectual property rights
LIK   Library, information and knowledge
IWM   Imperial War Museums
LACA   Libraries and Archives Copyright Alliance
PET   privacy-enhancing technology
RRS   records retention schedule
SAR   subject access request

TDM	text and data mining
TPM	technological protection measure
UK IPO	UK Intellectual Property Office
WATCH	Writers Artists and their Copyright Holders

List of figures and tables

Figures

Tables

List of case studies

Introduction

This book provides an overview of important information law issues for library, information and knowledge (hereinafter LIK) workers. Focusing specifically on copyright and other intellectual property rights (IPR), freedom of information (FoI), and data protection, the book is based upon UK law as of November 2019. The relevant laws in other countries sometimes differ a bit from UK law, sometimes a lot, and this fact should be borne in mind by readers. LIK workers need to know about these areas of law, both because their organisations must comply with the law and because this knowledge provides them with tools when responding to user enquiries. For example, knowledge of what can be obtained by use of freedom of information legislation can be extremely helpful to users. Thus LIK workers, often at the front line of managing and monitoring their organisation's legal compliance, have roles and responsibilities in both complying with the law and taking advantage of its provisions from time to time.

On a broader level, information law issues dovetail together, creating a sophisticated, complex and delicate balance between facilitating open and free access to information – thus supporting open and accountable government, democratic freedom and an uncensored press – simultaneously with the necessity for control and privacy. This balance is not always successfully achieved, which can result in tension and sometimes legal cases and court judgments. Information law tries to achieve this balance by creating clarity about what is definitely legal or illegal, whilst providing exemptions and exceptions and room for interpretation, risk management and the user's own 'gut feeling' by the frequent use of terms such as 'reasonable', 'fair' and 'justifiable'. LIK workers are operating in a constantly changing digital space in which everyone is often simultaneously a content creator, publisher and user.

This makes the interpretation and application of laws that are steeped in hundreds of years of historical tradition challenging. Moreover, the interplay between legal compliance and ethics is complex: often the two follow the same trajectory, but occasionally, ethical considerations, such as the specific nature of content, might preclude its use even if there are very few or no legal compliance issues. Material associated with war and conflict from the First World War is one such example. Similarly, material collected from recent anti-government protests might pose relative substantive provenance and/or copyright/data privacy issues, but collecting and using it ensures that our organisations do not self-censor important (historic) events.

To do their jobs, LIK workers need not only to understand the law, but also to develop the skills, confidence and organisational policy frameworks to apply the law's principles to their context of use. They need the knowledge and skills to help them decide what is acceptable and to develop appropriate risk-aware approaches when things, as they often can be, are not clear. As a result, the issue of risk within the context of legal compliance is a central theme of this book and there is therefore a focus on how LIK workers can achieve the appropriate balance between compliance and pragmatism.

For too long, however, information law has been viewed through a purely legal compliance lens. Often given as an excuse for inactivity because of its complexity, information law has sometimes languished, been side-lined, ignored or feared and, as a result, has not necessarily been embedded within routine organisational processes. Fear has also meant that it has not always been integrated into organisational policies, practices, project planning and resource management. This can manifest itself in a lack of basic staff training or expected competences of staff and, ultimately, risk aversion. Many librarianship and information science degree courses include modules covering key aspects of information law, but not every LIK worker has completed such modules and/or they may have learned about these topics many years ago, and/or they have not been trained in its practical, day-to-day implementation. Instead, some organisations have overly relied upon external consultants and/or legal professionals who are brought in to correct things that should have never gone wrong in the first place. Furthermore, we would argue that sometimes the mismanagement and marginalisation of information law within organisations has impacted negatively on the healthy functioning of the LIK sector. This is because ultimately a lack of understanding hampers the optimisation of the access and use of important resources. This has resulted in some specific issues, which have included:

◆ the denial of key skills development for staff, such as negotiation skills in order to broker the best deals for their organisations with suppliers of resources, or skills in understanding and responding to data protection challenges

◆ overly risk-averse positions in terms of resource use and access or self-censoring by choosing to provide access (whether digital publishing or otherwise) to only that information which presents no risks at all and thus skewing access to information

◆ a reduction in the ability of organisations to deal as efficiently as they could with rights clearance

◆ duplication of costs when organisations may be paying more than once for access to the same resources

◆ the haemorrhaging of rights in works created by volunteers, interns, freelancers and contractors, when organisations fail to secure the necessary transfer of copyright or permissions to reuse such works

◆ organisations not prepared to consider the fundamental role of risk management and subsequently not considering how risks might be mitigated in all kinds of situations

◆ overly risk-averse, or too slapdash, approaches when collecting or handling personal data

◆ sometimes not even understanding that what the organisation is collecting or handling is indeed personal data

◆ creating, destroying or amending materials when they should not be created or so dealt with, for example failing to consider moral rights when amending materials, or failing to consider data protection law when destroying records

◆ failure to understand that data held by the organisation (if it is a government or other official body) is potentially subject to inspection under freedom of information legislation

◆ failure to understand the rights organisations have to undertake text and data mining on digital materials held by third parties

◆ failure to understand terms such as 'substantial', 'reasonable', 'fair', 'justifiable' and 'non-commercial' in copyright and database right law.

The management of these issues is important because staff members are likely to encounter many types of digital (born digital and digital surrogates) as well as paper-based resources capable of being created, held or used by their institutions under various terms and conditions. How these resources can be used, and possibly repurposed, by whom, where, when and for how long needs to be properly managed. Partnerships or other types of relationship between branches of the same organisation (including those which are international), or between the organisation and other organisations, add to the complexities, and thereby muddy the waters considerably regarding resource access and use.

All this means that LIK workers need to understand and communicate to others within the context of all resources, whether old-established or being newly created, what rights their institution owns, those that it does not and those where rights holders are unknown or cannot be traced. They also need to understand what rights third parties have in respect of those resources. For example, LIK workers should understand and communicate whether certain resources may be subject to freedom of information requests, what rights under data protection law individuals have to inspect data held by the organisation about them, and what rights such data subjects have to demand rectification of errors or deletion of personal data held about them. LIK workers also need to understand and communicate what rights anyone has to complain about the way data relevant to their needs is being held, disseminated or exploited. Furthermore, where necessary, they will need to understand the vital role of risk management, how permissions can be sought and from whom, what to do if permissions cannot be obtained, as well as under what terms resources can then be accessed and then possibly used, amended or repurposed.

Fathoming out what can be done with different types of resources derived from multiple sources, often with layers of associated rights and permissions, can be daunting even for those well versed in copyright, data protection and licensing. This is in part due to the quantities of resources and their licences encountered by LIK workers, but also in part due to the many possibilities of blending different digital resources together, thereby repurposing them in a variety of ways. Staff members also need to understand the role of Creative Commons (CC) licences and how they can use them to achieve open access and embed them within broader organisational licensing and business strategies.

Some organisations have adopted an approach whereby these issues can be dealt with on a localised basis. In fact, the ramifications of information law are an organisation-wide issue that impact upon the creation, use, access to and reuse of all information resources and therefore needs to be treated as an issue that needs organisation-wide policies and staff who are trained, and confident in, all aspects of information law. This book aims to deal with some of these issues by bringing information law in from the cold, recognising that it raises multi-faceted organisational issues that are way beyond the types of matters dealt with by compliance officers. Indeed, the management of information law requires a top-down *and* bottom-up approach. In other words, what is required is an approach where staff awareness is supported by senior management buy-in and championing. This, in turn, implies a symbiotic environment where staff on the ground are well versed in the organisation's long-term strategy and policies, are trained to think in strategic ways, and have the confidence to make suggestions and recommendations to senior management and to point out where the organisation is not acting correctly. It also implies that staff have the confidence to understand that often the issues raised involve risk management, and that an appropriate balance between total risk avoidance and high-risk approaches is necessary. The precise balance depends, of course, on the type of organisation involved, its size, reputation, the costs of proposed compliance activities, the structure of the organisation, its governance and core strategic objectives and other factors. However, it is also important to be realistic. The changes that we face in the workplace, good and bad, bring uncertainty and worry – and so how can we help our staff build knowledge in traditionally more complicated issues like copyright, data protection and FoI? How can we develop and grow their knowledge in these areas, whilst also helping them feel safe to take proportionate risks?

This book is therefore divided into the following subsequent chapters, based on our 'Compliance methodology' (see Figure 0.1 on the next page). This is a tried and tested methodology, developed and used by us, to help LIK workers to understand the legal issues that are central to the information they hold or that they wish to access, and then establish a framework so that their organisation can both comply with their legal responsibilities and support, where appropriate, a suitably risk-aware environment which optimises access and use.

Chapters 1, 2 and 3 provide an introduction to UK law on copyright and related rights, data protection and freedom of information. These are the

Governance

Forward Plans

Policies

Procedures

Tools, Systems, Standards

Training and Awareness

Figure 0.1 *Compliance methodology*

three main areas of information law that apply to LIK services. Other areas of law, of course, could be relevant in some situations, such as the laws of confidentiality, defamation, obscenity, etc., but these are less likely to arise in library, information and knowledge services that often only deal with formally published information. Chapter 4 is an introduction to information law governance, which is discussed in the broader context of information governance, and forward plans. This chapter defines information governance and the need for information law to be embedded in organisational policies and procedures. It also addresses the need for the top-down, bottom-up approach to ensure that an appropriate organisational framework is developed, based on knowledge and input of both senior officers in an organisation and the staff implementing policy at an operational level. Chapter 5 addresses the need for information law policies and provides checklists for the content of such policies, considering the overlaps between different laws and how to resolve the tensions between them that arise in practice. Appendices 1 and 2 provide example policies. Chapters 6, 7 and 8 focus on putting policies into practice through organisational procedures, including copyright, data and information audits, asset and record registers, referring to sources of guidance provided on required procedures and documenting activities. Chapter 9 identifies and discusses practical tools, systems and standards that can be used in

LIK services, and organisations more generally, as part of putting procedures into practice. Chapter 10 explores the crucial role of awareness and training for staff and other organisational stakeholders. Without this awareness and training, staff will lack the confidence to engage and deal skilfully with information law issues and compliance requirements, including finding the appropriate balance in risk management. Chapter 11, the final substantive chapter in this book, speculates about the future and challenges faced by LIK workers, making the case for lobbying by our community to make information law more relevant and helpful in the future.

In conclusion: if the matters discussed in this book are being dealt with appropriately in an organisation, there will be less need to call in outside experts to put things right because mistakes are much less likely to have occurred. All three authors of this book, who have collective experience of over 100 years in information law compliance, undertake external consultancy work using the framework outlined in this book in the field of information law, and sometimes advise on how a problematic situation should be resolved. We, and fellow external experts, might not be happy to lose business as a result of readers following the advice and information in this book, but you, the readers, should be!

1

Copyright and related rights

Introduction

Copyright is the exclusive and assignable legal right, initially given to the author of an original work for a fixed number of years, to reproduce, print, publish, disseminate electronically, perform, or record their creative material. The word 'initially' is used, as the author can and often does assign the copyright, i.e. transfer the copyright ownership, to a third party, such as a publisher. Assignment is discussed further below. In order to use copyright materials, you have to know what it is and the difficulties and opportunities copyright can create.

In the UK, copyright law is primarily based on the Copyright, Designs and Patents Act 1988 and subsequent revisions, including the Copyright and Related Rights Regulations 2003, SI 2003/2498, various Copyright Rights in Performances Regulations 2014, some sections of previous Copyright Acts 1911 and 1956, various European Union (EU) Directives (most of which have been transposed into UK law by means of Statutory Instruments), international treaties that the UK has signed up to and case law from UK Courts and the European Court of Justice (ECJ).[1] The key points to note about copyright are as follows:

◆ Copyright is an economic right granted exclusively to the creator(s) of an original work, which must be in some tangible or fixed format, to either permit or to prevent other people from copying, and doing

---

1. At the time this book was written, the UK was still a member of the European Union and ECJ decisions applied to it. If the UK does leave the EU, future ECJ decisions will not automatically apply in the UK, though in practice, we expect UK courts will often still follow the decisions taken by the ECJ.

certain other things (known as 'restricted acts' – see further discussion below), to it. If someone does carry out a restricted act on a copyright work without permission, they may have infringed the copyright, and the copyright owner is entitled to sue in a civil court case and seek forms of redress, such as damages for loss of income, destruction of infringing copies, etc. There are also certain circumstances where carrying out or enabling infringement becomes a criminal offence.

◆ In most countries of the world, including the UK, copyright is automatic. In other words, there are no formalities one has to go through, or fees to be paid, to acquire copyright.

◆ Copyright does not protect an idea, but it can protect the material expression of the idea.

◆ Works are protected regardless of their merit, although they need to be original (i.e. not copied from something else) and show some level of skill and judgement in their creation.[2]

◆ Notwithstanding the above statements, third parties *can* under some circumstances carry out restricted acts on all or part of a copyright work without a problem. These so-called exceptions to copyright are discussed further below.

◆ The lifetime of copyright varies depending on circumstances, but for many materials it lasts a long time – at least to the end of the 50 years *after* the death of the creator and often to the end of 70 years *after* the death. When the person dies, ownership of the copyright normally passes to their heirs and successors. Once copyright in a work has expired, anyone can do what they like with the original work.

◆ Copyright works can be created by an individual, a team of individuals (in which case they jointly own the copyright), or by an organisation, such as a limited company, where typically the copyright in works created by an employee as part of their normal employee duties are automatically owned by the employer. It is worth noting, however, that custom and practice in some organisations, such as higher education institutions (HEIs), means that employee-created works are often treated as if they belong to the employee, rather than by the employing institution.

◆ The ownership of copyright in a work can be, and often is,

---

2. If need be, a court would have to decide if sufficient skill or judgement had been used, and/or whether the item had been copied from another item.

transferred to a third party (often for money). This is known as assignment. Thus, frequently a creator will assign their copyright to a publisher in return for a single payment or for royalties. This does not affect the lifetime of the copyright, but does of course affect its ownership. An alternative to assignment is the granting of a licence. In this case, the creator retains ownership of the copyright, but grants permission to the person(s) or organisation(s) licensed to carry out one or more restricted acts on all or part of the work. Licences are often charged for, but some are free of charge. Notable examples of the latter are the CC licences.[3] There are three types of licence: an exclusive licence is one granted to a single entity, with the promise no similar licence will be granted to anyone else; a sole licence is one where just a single third party plus the original creator are allowed to exploit the copyright; and a non-exclusive licence is where the owner does not guarantee that others may not also obtain the licence.

The UK is one of hundreds of countries[4] that have signed international copyright conventions, most notably the Berne Convention.[5] This means that any creator in any of those countries automatically gets copyright protection in the UK for their works, and any UK creator automatically gets protection for their works in the other signatory countries. However, we don't have one single copyright law covering these countries, but rather a variety of similar, but not identical laws. Even the laws of EU member states are not identical. The key principles are the same but there are often significant variations in different countries' copyright laws.

What does copyright protect?

Copyright only protects certain categories of things specified by legislation. If a resource does not fall within one of the categories, it will not be protected by copyright. These categories are:

◆ Literary works, which include any combination of words and numbers, in all languages, as well as lyrics to songs, software, and

---

3. https://creativecommons.org/licenses
4. For an up-to-date list of signatories, see https://copyrighthouse.co.uk/copyright/countries-berne-convention.htm
5. www.wipo.int/treaties/en/ip/berne

newspaper articles. These are protected in the UK and many other countries for the creators' lifetime plus 70 years. For unpublished works by known authors, the copyright lasts longer – you should check legal texts for the details. There is no implication of literary merit, so even a poorly written school child's essay is considered to be a literary work. A single word never enjoys copyright (though there may be trademarks associated with it), but a single sentence may well do. Database rights (see below) may also apply to sets of words and/or numbers.

◆ Artistic works, including photos (whether stored electronically, printed, or displayed on e.g. Facebook), paintings, maps, drawings and etchings and sculptures. These are protected for the originator's lifetime plus 70 years. Crown copyright, however, is protected for 50 years from the end of the year of creation (this would apply to e.g. maps and stamps). Ordnance Survey[6] usually grants usage rights to third parties if requested.

◆ Music – sheet music copyright lasts for the creator's lifetime plus 70 years and sound recordings are covered for 70 years from creation.

◆ Typographic arrangement protects the layout of printed documentation, books, reproductions of other people's works, reprinting, newspapers, etc. This copyright lasts for 25 years from the end of the year of creation.

◆ Broadcasts, including TV or radio; the copyright for these last for 50 years from the end of the year of the first broadcast.

◆ Films – the copyright term for these is lifetime plus 70 years of the last of those who helped create the film, i.e., the director, producer, script writer or composer (including the person who wrote the lyrics) to die.

◆ Dramatic works – anything that can be enacted, performance art, the choreography of a ballet, plays, dance, etc. The copyright lasts for the lifetime of the creator plus 70 years.

These categories are defined more fully in the legislation. Note that, because copyright is an automatic right, there is no need to use the copyright symbol © in the UK to get protection, though it is often handy

---

6. In 2013, the Ordnance Survey became a Government-owned limited company and has asserted copyright for the lifetime of its employees plus 70 years from the end of the year that they died.

to include it to advertise the fact that the owner knows about copyright and is willing to assert their rights. Note also that many creations will involve a combination of different copyright categories. For example, in the case of books, there are potentially at least three categories of copyright:

◆ in the cover, which is probably an artistic work (lifetime plus 70 years) and may also be a literary work if the book title is lengthy
◆ in the text, which is a literary work (lifetime plus 70 years)
◆ the typographic arrangement; when publishers re-print, they will often change the typographic arrangement. They can obtain copyright in the new layout (25 years from creation)
◆ there may well also be photographs or drawings in the book (more artistic works), or musical notation may be included.

Restricted acts

These are the acts carried out on a copyright work that would be infringement if an exception to copyright (see below) did not apply. They are as follows:

◆ The copyright owner has the exclusive right to copy, or to authorise others to copy, all or a substantial[7] part of the work, whatever the medium. This includes manual transcription, photocopying, tracing, and all types of scanning or other digitisation.
◆ The copyright owner has the exclusive right to issue, or to authorise others to issue, one or more copies of the work to the public.[8] Whether the copies are free of charge or charged for is irrelevant when deciding if infringement has taken place. This restricted act does not, however, prevent the sale of, for example, second-hand books.
◆ The copyright owner has the exclusive right to rent or lend, or to authorise a third party to rent or lend, certain types of works to the public. Rental means charging for the lending, whilst lending is for free. Libraries have special dispensations regarding lending, and the loan of a book to a friend would not be considered infringement.
◆ The copyright owner has the exclusive right to 'communicate the work to the public', or to authorise someone else to do so. This term

---

7. What is, or is not, considered 'substantial' is something courts have to decide.
8. What is, or is not 'the public', again is something courts would have to decide.

covers all types of electronic transmission, e.g. through the internet, or transmission by broadcasting.

◆ Finally, the copyright owner has the exclusive right to adapt, or authorise others to adapt, some types of copyright work.

Case study 1.1: Ethel Bilborough's diary

Ethel Bilborough was a journalist and artist who wrote a personal diary during the outbreak of the First World War. Her hand-written diary is now owned by the Imperial War Museums (IWM) in London. This is primarily the copyright story of how Ethel's diary became a hardback book published by Ebury Press, in association with IWM, and currently available from Amazon.[9] Whilst there is seemingly a massive difference between the rights issues associated with a diary written over 100 years ago and the digital age of today, the parallels are striking. Ethel's diary includes a number of her sketches. She also used the diary as a scrapbook and cut things out and pasted them in, including an envelope, which had been opened by the official wartime censor, newspaper cuttings, stamps, etc. The original diary was donated to the IWM some years ago, but at the time of acces-sion, neither a copyright transfer (assignment) nor a licence had been sought. Ethel died in the 1950s. Because her diary was not published in her lifetime, the duration of copyright in unpublished works under UK copyright law lasts until the end of the year 2039. IWM's contractual obligations to Ebury Press, copyright compliance and ethical drivers were clear: copyright permission had to be sought.

Ethel did not have a digital footprint, so IWM got hold of both her will and that of her husband, Kenneth Bilborough. Ethel died before Kenneth and he married his secretary Elsie. Elsie did not leave a will but had a living heir: Ethel's husband's second wife's niece owned the copyright in the diary! IWM secured a transfer of copyright from the niece, but that was not the end of the story. The next issue IWM faced when reproducing Ethel's diary was how to deal with all of the additional material she stuck into her diary from outside sources. IWM spent a great deal of time researching all the different items within the diary, finding out who produced them and asking their permission to use them. Using Image Recognition Software such as Tin Eye, Foto Forensics and Google Image Search, IWM managed to identify the sources of the commercially licensed content and requested the necessary permissions.

Far from being irrelevant, the copyright story of Ethel Bilborough's diary

---

9. www.amazon.co.uk/War-Diary-1914-1918-Ethel-Bilbrough/dp/0091951119

presents some fascinating insights into contemporary copyright issues associated with the digital age:

1   Ethel cut and pasted materials created by other people into her diary as we copy/cut and paste digital content into digital resources. The copyright issues associated with these layers of third-party rights will be similar.
2   Time and resources are needed to identify, research and clear these rights.
3   Copyright is a business-critical issue: weighing up the costs, versus the benefits, versus the risks.
4   This story illustrates the need to consider copyright at the point of acquisition/commissioning of any type of content, whether print or digital. Without clear written agreements, materials might be acquired or commissioned but cannot be used. This lack of efficiency in rights clearance can have an impact on profit margin for commercial products if rights are not dealt with at the correct time.
5   It is very important that copyright and licensing commitments in any contracts with third parties, such as publishers and funding bodies, are identified and acted upon. For example, funders are likely to expect you to seek permissions for the content to be published and possibly under certain specific licensing conditions (such as CC licences).

Exceptions to copyright

There are some specified exceptions to copyright, listed below, which allow any third party to do a restricted act with someone else's work so long as the use does not conflict with the normal exploitation of the work by the rights owner. In general, such exceptions apply irrespective of the wishes of the copyright owner, so any licence or other statement made by a copyright owner stating that one cannot carry out such acts is invalid in law and can be ignored. Consider, for example, this statement: 'No part of this book may be reprinted or reproduced or utilised in any form or by any electronic, mechanical or other means, now known or hereafter invented, including photocopying and recording, or in any information storage or retrieval system, without permission from the publishers'. This statement appears in a textbook on publishing law (Jones and Benson, 2016). Such misleading statements are, unfortunately, all too common. To make such a statement accurate, it should be preceded by the words 'Other than as permitted by law . . .'.

Exceptions to copyright should be viewed in the light of public interest and the greater good. These are exemplified in copyright legislation and were updated in 2014 (more about the 2014 changes later). The major exceptions are for the following purposes:

- so-called fair dealing for non-commercial research or private study, for criticism or review, for quotation, for news reporting, or for caricature/parody/pastiche
- copying for the purpose of text or data mining, which is discussed further below
- copying for people with disabilities
- rental or lending of the work by certain permitted organisations
- educational purposes
- public administration
- private copying
- copying carried out by libraries, museums or archives for their patrons, or for interlibrary loan purposes
- copying in response to FoI requests, or other legal obligations.

There are other exceptions, as well, which provide a relatively comprehensive framework of uses. It should be noted that each one of these exceptions has rules associated with it, and readers should check legal texts or the original legislation to understand what is, or is not, allowed. Ultimately many of the exceptions to copyright are underpinned by the concept of 'fair dealing', which is undefined in the legislation. This means that user needs to consider what is reasonable, asking themselves 'how would I feel if it were my work that were being used for that purpose, in that way?' i.e. what would be fair?

It is important to note that it is never infringement to copy from a work that is out of copyright, or to copy an insubstantial part of an in-copyright work, though 'insubstantial' is a subjective concept and would be subject to decisions by a court regarding what is, or is not, substantial. There are special rules relating to unpublished works, such as private letters and diaries, and so-called 'orphan works', i.e., works that are in copyright but one cannot identify who the copyright owner is. Again, if you have to deal with such works, you should consult standard texts on copyright law.

The new text and data mining exception

In 2014, the UK government introduced a number of changes to copyright law. Amongst those changes was one relating to text and data mining (TDM), introducing a new exception to copyright, i.e., giving users permission to do things relating to TDM that were previously legally uncertain or prohibited. TDM involves making copies of copyright works (typically scholarly publications and data, but by no means always such materials – it could be the full text of a politician's speeches, for example, for the purpose of analysing their use of words and phrases, the consistency of their policies, etc.). The exception, incorporated in the Copyright, Designs and Patents Act 1988, s. 29A, allows researchers to make copies of any copyright material for the purpose of 'computational analysis' (i.e. TDM) if they already have 'lawful access' to said materials, for example because the researcher (or their employer) has purchased or subscribed to the in-copyright materials. This exception only permits the making of copies for TDM for non-commercial research.

The exception permits any published and unpublished in-copyright works to be copied for the purpose of TDM. This includes sound, film/video, artistic works, journal articles, textual materials, tables and databases, as well as data. It overrides any contractual term that states you cannot undertake such copying and analysis. This all sounds great, but there are two important caveats. The first is that the research that needs the TDM approach must be non-commercial. This does not exclude commercial bodies from taking advantage of the exception, but only under restricted circumstances. Commercial organisations can use the exception only if the research in question is for non-commercial purposes. Equally, a not-for-profit organisation such as a university cannot take advantage of the exception if the research in question is for a commercial purpose, e.g. with the intention of selling the results of the analysis. However, 'non-commercial' is not defined in the legislation or by case law: for instance, what if a university researcher is doing the research which is partly or fully funded by a for-profit company, which will have access to the results of the research and may well use those results to launch new commercial products?

The second caveat relates to potential damage to a vendor's online system, such as digital access to the full text of a range of journals. The exception states: 'Publishers and content providers are able to apply reasonable measures to maintain their network security or stability.'

Although the exception also states that 'these measures should not prevent or unreasonably restrict a researcher's ability to text and data mine' (Intellectual Property Office, 2014), in practice many publishers have imposed limits on how much can be downloaded for TDM purposes. We have yet to see any clear evidence from a publisher showing that TDM activities do slow down their systems, and suspect their rules imposing limits are designed to frustrate researchers. As it would be unlawful to try to bypass any such measures imposed by publishers, researchers, and librarians who maintain such subscriptions on behalf of their users, are very reluctant to permit heavy TDM activities. In our view, researchers and librarians are being unnecessarily nervous of antagonising publishers on this issue by refusing to challenge limits imposed, but in practice, the new exception has not helped researchers as much as was originally hoped. The European Union (EU) introduced a TDM exception by means of Council Directive (EC) 2019/790 on copyright and related rights in the Digital Single Market and amending Directives 96/9/EC and 2001/29/EC [2019] OJ L130. However, the Directive's wording appears to be more restrictive than the UK's exception.

Moral rights

In addition to copyright, there are three other closely related rights – moral rights, database rights and performers' rights. Moral rights relate to the creator's honour or reputation. They give the creator:

◆ the right to be named as the creator of the work (paternity right)
◆ the right to object to someone being wrongly identified as the creator of a work which the person did not create (false attribution right)
◆ the right to object to derogatory treatment of the work (derogatory treatment right, also known as the right of integrity).

Moral rights can't be assigned to anyone else (unlike copyright), but they can be waived. Individuals might be put under pressure by, say, distributors and/or publishers, to waive any moral rights they might hold in relation to something they have created. A better approach in our view is to ask the creator for consent to edit something and/or attribute when reasonably practicable. This is an important, more ethical and 'softer' alternative to asking the creator to waive their moral rights. The right to object to derogatory treatment can, in some cases, overlap with the law of defamation, as derogatory treatment might involve changing the work in such a way as to impugn the reputation of the original creator, such as quoting them out of context to give a misleading impression of what they created. Most moral rights in the UK last as long as copyright does, i.e., typically 70 years after the death of the creator. After the creator's death, their moral rights are inherited by the creator's personal representative. The right relating to false attribution only lasts for 20 years after the creator's death. If anyone infringes moral rights, the owner of the rights can sue them. There have not been many such cases in practice, though that might be because users of copyright materials have been very cautious about their use of such materials. As there are exceptions to the right, you need to check legal textbooks regarding whether moral rights might apply in particular circumstances. A risk assessment needs to be made when dealing with a third party's moral rights (other chapters in the book discuss risk management).

Database rights

The Copyright, Designs and Patents Act 1988, s. 3A defines a database as 'a collection of independent works, data or other materials arranged in a systematic or methodical way and individually accessible by electronic or other means'. The database does not have to be electronic – it could be a collection of printed items, photographs, and so on. Even a very modest collection of (say) a dozen items could be considered a database in law. There is no requirement that each individual item enjoys copyright.

In UK law, as in other EU member states,[10] databases can be protected in one or both of two ways. They may be protected by copyright as literary works, and/or database rights may protect them. There is also a group of databases that enjoy no protection at all, as we shall see. To enjoy copyright protection as a literary work, the database must be original – not copied from somewhere else – and it must show some level of creativity by reason of the selection or arrangement of the contents of the database. As with other literary works, the author is the person who created the database. If, as is often the case, employees create the database as part of their employee duties, then the employer is normally the owner of the resulting database.

---

10. Database rights were introduced following an EU Directive, and the law is broadly similar in each EU member state. Only a few non-EU countries have adopted the concept of database right.

Note that such a database can only be copyright as a literary work, but not an artistic work or any of the other types of copyright work. Thus, a collection of artistic works, sound recordings, TV programmes and so on cannot enjoy copyright in the collection, though they can enjoy database right. To enjoy database right, the collection can comprise multiple works in any medium, not just words and numbers, and there is no requirement for any creativity. However, to enjoy database right, there must have been substantial investment in obtaining, verifying or presenting the contents of the database. The key issue at stake here, as identified in some major ECJ decisions, is that irrespective of how much effort went into the research that led to the data being made, if the database fails the above criteria, it cannot get database right. Thus, the substantial investment refers to the resources expended to seek out pre-existing data and/or verifying their accuracy and/or collating and then presenting them, but does not extend to the primary creation of the contents of the database itself.

Case study 1.2: ECJ case British Horseracing Board Ltd v. William Hill Organisation Ltd

British Horseracing Board Ltd (BHB) sued William Hill Ltd, the well-known firm of bookmakers, for using parts of its database of horses and jockeys who were going to race in future races, without paying a licence fee. This case was decided in 2005. There was no claim of copyright infringement, as the BHB acknowledged implicitly that there had been no intellectual creativity involved in making the master database – it was simply a comprehensive database of runners, jockeys, owners and so on. The case was about infringement of database right. The ECJ decided that there was no database right in these details because the BHB had already created the database for quite different purposes (the general management of UK horse-racing), and no particular resource had gone into the obtaining, verification or display of the contents of the database that it was licensing to other bookmakers for a fee.

To enjoy database right, significant effort must have been expended on things other than the creation of the original data and so a database that just happens to spin out of some other activity will not enjoy database rights. The owner of database right is the individual or organisation that did the obtaining, verifying or presenting the contents of the database.

Performers' rights

The performer enjoys some rights relating to a performance, which includes dramatic performance, dance, mime, musical performance, a reading or a variety act. A lecture will also count as a performance. It is irrelevant whether the material being performed is in copyright or not, the protection is for the performance of the work. The performers' rights are infringed if, without the performer's consent, someone records all or a substantial part of the performance, or broadcasts it. If the recording is sold, distributed (whether for a fee or not), or the copy is rented or lent out or is in any way disseminated electronically without permission, again this is infringement of the performer's rights. Incidentally, there are also moral rights in performances. As with other rights, if more than one person is involved in a performance, they share ownership of those rights. Performers' rights usually last for 50 years from the end of the year of the performance. There are some limited exceptions to the rights for libraries and archives.

Some problems arising from copyright

If someone carries out some commissioned work for you, be it a photographer, someone delivering workshops or training, etc., they automatically own the rights to their work unless they have signed a contract assigning copyright to the person who commissioned the work. It is important when commissioning anyone to do anything that you get them to sign a contract about how the work will be used and what you expect from them.

You can control the content on your own site, the terms under which you publish items onto your site and the terms and conditions under which other people use your material or contribute their own content to your site. However, when posting your material to a third-party site, e.g., Wikipedia, Twitter or Facebook, you must abide by that site's terms and conditions which you have signed up to, and third parties will be able to use your material in any way compatible with those terms. The terms and conditions you sign up to when you put something on another platform broadly reflect classic publishing agreements and thus typically are as follows:

1 It is assumed that you own the rights to the item you are posting.
2 You grant the publisher and everyone who has signed up to use that

site a (typically free of charge non-exclusive) licence to use your content. There are probably other issues, such as potential loss of privacy, but these are outside the remit of this chapter.

3   You accept all the risks, responsibilities and liability if you are not the rights holder and do not have the necessary permissions to offer the materials you are posting.

4   You accept all the risks and liability for the legality of the materials you are posting, e.g. that they are not defamatory, or break any law, such as those relating to national security, prevention of terrorism, official secrets or data protection.

Consider Facebook – as soon as you sign up to it, you enter into a contractual agreement which gives it rights, especially in the case of photographs, to reuse your postings and even to pass them on to third-party organisations such as Getty Images for commercial purposes. So although Facebook can be a great way to connect with new audiences, you need to make sure you read its terms and conditions carefully and weigh up the risks, disadvantages and benefits.

If you are posting other peoples' works on social media platforms, consider the following:

◆   Do you have permission to do so?
◆   Don't do it if you feel it is ethically, legally or contractually high risk.
◆   Use a risk management approach, including a risk mitigation strategy (see Chapters 7, 8 and 9 on risk management, and on contracts and licensing procedures, tools and templates).

Orphan works

These are works where you may or may not know who the person is who created the works but you can't trace the rights holder. The copyright for published orphan works usually lasts for the lifetime of the person who created it plus 70 years after their death. If you don't know who created the work, you should make a reasonable guess as to the age of the work and likely age of the creator, and then make a working assumption on likely expiry of copyright. We suggest an estimate of 100 years after the creation of the work would be realistic for most cases of orphan works where you know who created it but not when they died. Copyright in the case of orphan works that are anonymous, or in unpublished works, expires in 2039, unless they were published or first made available to the public after 1969, in which case their copyright expires 70 years after such creation, or publication. Options for using orphan works are:

◆ Make an informed guess as to when copyright is likely to expire/has expired. Carry out a risk management exercise on the item. Don't use the item if you think it is too risky.

◆ Buy a licence to use it from the UK Intellectual Property Office (go onto the IPO website).[11] This applies to the UK only and lasts for up to seven years so is not appropriate if you plan to disseminate the work outside the UK, which would include online publishing, and is not appropriate if you wish to use the item for longer than seven years. Because of these limitations, relatively few such licences have been applied for.

◆ At the time of writing there is a EU Orphan Works exception which can be used by libraries, archives, museums, educational establishments and public broadcasts for text-based works and audiovisual works (films, sound recordings), but not for photos. You can put these works online even if they are not out of copyright. However, this EU-initiated exception will not continue in the UK if and when it leaves the EU, particularly without a deal.

You can find more information on orphan works licensing in Chapters 7 and 9. These are the only choices available, and they only offer limited help for most situations where orphan works arise.

It cannot be stressed too much that *handling copyright problems is as much to do with management of risk, as it is to do with the law*. Risk management is crucial in deciding whether to use something that is in (or is likely to be in) copyright and for which you don't have permissions. There are three parts to risk management strategy: calculation of the risks; the cost/benefit calculation; and your (or your employer's) appetite for risk. Of course, knowledge of the law is needed but, as has already been noted in this book, there are too many vague words (such as 'substantial', 'the public' 'normal exploitation', 'commercial', 'reasonable', etc.) employed in the legislation and by courts for certainty regarding a particular use to arise. Copyright

---

11. www.gov.uk/guidance/copyright-orphan-works#before-you-apply-for-a-licence

law is not always black and white and if, for example, significant efforts have been made to trace the copyright owner, and this can be backed up with evidence, then it is up to the organisation to calculate the risk and decide if this is mitigated by the research it has undertaken. It is important to make sure that the cost of obtaining copyright or licensed use does not exceed the benefit of using the item. When there are several layers of copyright to assess, or large amounts of research needed to establish, for example, who the owner of the copyright is, there are costs in terms of time as well as monetary value.

It is important to have a strategy towards risk: how risk-aware and how risk-averse are you/your organisation? For an organisation, being risk-aware requires a corporate decision about the organisation's approach to risk decided by the senior management team. However, you always need to have a notice and take-down procedure (see Chapter 6), so that items can, for example, be taken down immediately from a website if there is an issue. This is, of course, not so easy in the case of printed publications. You need to record all the processes you undertook before reproducing any given potentially problematic item. All the types of rights listed above, and not just copyright, need to be considered. And make sure you or your employer has appropriate indemnity insurance to cover it and you for any claims. Being risk-averse means that you will need to put a lot more effort in to trying to trace rights holders, for example; it involves checking things online, contacting organisations who might be able to help, etc. For some organisations, reputational risk is more important than financial risk, of course.

Managing copyright

If something is in copyright and you or your organisation do not own the copyright, there are various options if you wish to use a work:

1   Try to use the work under one of the exceptions to copyright.
2   Use the work under an existing licence, which can include CC licensed materials. The organisation may already be signed up to a relevant licensing scheme.
3   Make every effort to clear the rights, typically through a bespoke licence.
4   Take a risk-managed approach to using the item if, for example, you

cannot trace the rights holders, or you have traced them but they have not replied to enquiries.

In Chapter 6, we discuss in more detail the procedures that should be put in place to ensure legal compliance and effective protection and exploitation of an organisation's intellectual property, including:

1 developing thorough procedures and policy documentation about how to deal with copyright
2 building 'rights and risks by design' into all project and budget management, to ensure that rights and risks are considered as early as possible, preferably through the lenses of costs and benefits
3 developing a risk management strategy for dealing with copyright issues
4 developing and publicising a notice and take-down policy
5 ensuring that there are robust terms and conditions for the use of materials created in the organisation
6 communicating copyright policies and issues to both internal and external staff and ensuring that awareness about policies and procedures is included in staff training.

2 Data protection

Introduction

Most developed countries have at least a minimum level of data protection legislation in place. The USA is notable in having only limited protection at a federal level, although many states have introduced such legislation. Data protection is based upon the notion that every individual has some rights over information about them and that abuse of this information should be prevented. Data protection legislation is an important component of the legal compliance framework, whose ultimate objective is trying to achieve the appropriate balance between privacy and freedom. Typically, data protection legislation requires the following:

◆ Data controllers (those that are responsible for managing data about individuals) must register with a supervisory body if they currently, or plan to, use so-called 'personal data', and if those data can be searched or manipulated using the individual's name (or equivalent identifier).

◆ Data subjects (living identifiable individuals who have data about them stored and manipulated by third parties) have the right to know whether data is held about them, and inspect what information is held about them.

◆ Data subjects can sue for damage caused by inaccurate data about them, or for other breaches, such as unauthorised release of such data.

◆ Data controllers must abide by certain general principles and codes of practice.

◆ Data processors (anyone who handles personal data under

instructions from a data controller) have to follow similar rules to their controllers.

♦ There are exemptions for matters of national security, crime prevention, etc.

♦ There must be systems in place to prevent unauthorised access, deletion or amendment of records containing personal data.

However, some countries' legislation goes much further, for example:

♦ Data controllers must explicitly request the permission of data subjects before handling their personal data.

♦ Data subjects can insist that data about them is deleted.

♦ Data subjects shall be entitled to know to whom data about them has been passed, and where data about them has come from.

♦ No decisions about the data subject may be made purely relying on information obtained from personal data files.

In 2018, EU, including the UK, data protection law was amended because of the implementation of the Council Regulation (EC) 2016/679 on the protection of natural persons with regard to the processing of personal data and on the free movement of such data, and repealing Directive 95/46/EC (generally known as the General Data Protection Regulation, or GDPR). This change to UK law was done by means of a new Data Protection Act 2018. Data protection laws in the UK and elsewhere are not new. In fact they have been in place for some time. In the UK, there were Data Protection Acts in 1984 and 1998. However the speed of technological change and alignment of easy access to goods and services across the EU and internationally resulted in the need to substantially revise these out-of-date laws, replacing them with the more robust GDPR, ensuring not just EU compliance, but also international compliance (discussed later in this chapter in more detail).

If the UK leaves the EU, it will become a *third country* for the purposes of the transfer of personal data outside the EU. This may require an 'adequacy decision' by the European Commission (EC) on the suitability of the UK's data protection framework. The UK Government has indicated that a legally binding data protection agreement between the EU and the UK would be more appropriate than an 'adequacy finding'. Such an agreement would include the UK's data protection authority, the Information Commissioner's Office (ICO), having a seat on the European Data Protection Board (EDPB). The result of GDPR is very close alignment of data protection laws in all EU member states. What is clear is that whether or not Brexit occurs (and if so, in what 'flavour' of Brexit), GDPR will continue to apply to all UK-based organisations wishing to do business in the EU or wishing to exchange information with organisations based in the EU.

It is worth stressing the difference between EU Regulations and Directives. EU Regulations become immediately enforceable as law in all member states. In contrast, the much more common Directives need to go through a local legislative approval process, and may be subject to some amendment.

Some details about the UK's data protection law

The UK's data protection law is based upon certain data protection principles. According to the UK Government's website,[1] the principles relating to personal data (the term is defined below) are that personal data should be:

- used fairly, lawfully and transparently
- used for specified, explicit purposes
- used in a way that is adequate, relevant and limited to only what is necessary
- accurate and, where necessary, kept up to date
- kept for no longer than is necessary
- handled in a way that ensures appropriate security, including protection against unlawful or unauthorised processing, access, loss, destruction or damage.

Case study 2.1: Too much personal information

An employer required all staff (male and female) to declare their chest size on a form used for collecting data about new employees. When challenged, the employer stated that it needed this information so it could keep the right stocks of overalls for those employees doing dirty jobs, such as cleaning. But most employees, including staff in the library, did not do such jobs. The employer was

---

1. www.gov.uk/data-protection

found guilty of a breach of the GDPR Principles (see below) and had to develop a new form for white-collar employees.

There is even stronger legal protection for so-called sensitive personal data, which is defined as information about:

♦ race
♦ ethnic background
♦ political opinions
♦ religious beliefs
♦ trade union membership
♦ genetics
♦ biometrics (where used for identification)
♦ health
♦ sex life or sexual orientation.

Another principle prohibits the transfer of personal data to countries outside the EEA (the European Economic Area, i.e., the EU plus a few other European countries) that do not have 'an adequate level of protection'. Two questions follow: what is 'transfer', and what is 'an adequate level of protection'? Transfer includes the sending of the data abroad, whether in the form of paper, floppy discs, material on a portable computer, or sending the material by online means to a country outside the EEA. Placing material on a website and allowing people in other countries to access and download it was the subject of a European court case, which decided, perhaps surprisingly, that it was not 'transfer'. So transfer means deliberate exporting of the data. It makes no difference whether the transfer is to third parties outside one's own organisation, or to people abroad within the organisation. Therefore, staff carrying laptops and travelling from the UK to outside the EEA, and, whilst there, processing personal data held on the laptop are just as potentially problematic as the more obvious types of transfer.

As noted earlier, the USA at present has no federal data protection law. So, transfer to the USA is *prima facie* illegal. However, there are some circumstances where such transfers to non-EEA countries such as the USA are legal; they may take place if one or more of the following apply:

◆ Where the individual gives consent to the transfer. This consent would be on a case-by-case basis. A blanket agreement is unlikely to be acceptable.

◆ Where the transfer is necessary for the performance of a contract between the data subject and the controller.

◆ Where the data subject has requested the transfer as part of some pre-contractual arrangement.

◆ Where the data transfer is to fulfil a contract that is in the interests of the data subject (this would again be considered on a case-by-case basis).

◆ Where the transfer is necessary for important public interest grounds or for the fulfilment of legal claims.

◆ Where the transfer is to protect the vital interests (normally taken to mean health-related) of the data subject.

◆ Where the transfer is from a public register which is there to provide information to the public.

Transfers to non-approved countries are also acceptable if they are made on contractual terms that are 'of a kind approved by the Commissioner'. Good examples are so-called 'safe harbours' in non-EEA countries. These are organisations that commit to a set of privacy principles. Any data transferred is stored in the safe harbour and may not be transferred anywhere else (unless that, too, is a safe harbour). These may be acceptable to the ICO.

Case study 2.2: Data protection safe harbours

In November 2011, the Irish data protection authorities announced they would be carrying out an audit of Facebook's Irish offices following a complaint from a Facebook user. The complainant requested a copy of his personal data held by Facebook. On receipt, he discovered that he had previously deleted much of the data that was included, and consequently launched a media campaign, 'Europe vs. Facebook', aimed at forcing Facebook to abide by European data protection laws. The Irish data protection authorities became involved, as the location of the Facebook's international headquarters is Dublin. The complaint has since been bounced back and forth between the Irish High Court and the Court of Justice of the European Union. The CJEU overturned the safe harbour that allowed Facebook to move data from the EU to the USA despite the latter's less stringent data protection laws. The case has continued, shifting focus to the contractual clauses that Facebook, and many other businesses, started relying on after the safe harbour deal was proclaimed invalid.

The GDPR Principles also confirm that processing (defined below) of personal data is lawful only if and to the extent that at least one of the following applies:

1   the data subject has given consent to the processing of his or her personal data for one or more specific purposes
2   processing is necessary for the performance of a contract to which the data subject is party or in order to take steps at the request of the data subject prior to entering into a contract
3   processing is necessary for compliance with a legal obligation to which the controller is subject
4   processing is necessary in order to protect the vital interests of the data subject or of another natural person
5   processing is necessary for the performance of a task carried out in the public interest or in the exercise of official authority vested in the controller
6   processing is necessary for the purposes of the legitimate interests pursued by the controller or by a third party, except where such interests are overridden by the interests or fundamental rights and freedoms of the data subject which require protection of personal data, in particular where the data subject is a child.

Where processing is based on consent, the controller must be able to demonstrate that the data subject has consented to processing of his or her personal data. The data subject has the right to withdraw his or her consent at any time. The withdrawal of consent does not affect the lawfulness of processing based on consent before its withdrawal. It must be as easy to withdraw as to give consent.

The processing of the personal data of a child is lawful where the child is at least 16 years old. Where the child is below the age of 16 years, such processing is lawful only if and to the extent that consent is given or authorised by the holder of parental responsibility over the child.

Processing of personal data revealing racial or ethnic origin, political opinions, religious or philosophical beliefs, or trade union membership, and the processing of genetic data, biometric data for the purpose of uniquely identifying a natural person, data concerning health or data concerning a natural person's sex life or sexual orientation is prohibited. This does not apply if one of the following applies:

1   The data subject has given explicit consent to the processing of those personal data for one or more specified purposes, except where EU or member state law provides that the prohibition referred to may not be lifted by the data subject.
2   Processing is necessary for the purposes of carrying out the obligations and exercising specific rights of the controller or of the data subject in the field of employment and social security and social protection law in so far as it is authorised by EU or member state law.
3   Processing is necessary to protect the vital interests of the data subject or of another natural person where the data subject is physically or legally incapable of giving consent.
4   Processing is carried out in the course of its legitimate activities with appropriate safeguards by a foundation, association or any other not-for-profit body with a political, philosophical, religious or trade union aim and on condition that the processing relates solely to the members or to former members of the body or to persons who have regular contact with it in connection with its purposes and that the personal data is not disclosed outside that body without the consent of the data subjects.
5   Processing relates to personal data which are manifestly made public by the data subject.
6   Processing is necessary for the establishment, exercise or defence of legal claims or whenever courts are acting in their judicial capacity.
7   Processing is necessary for reasons of substantial public interest, on the basis of EU or member state law.
8   Processing is necessary for the purposes of preventive or occupational medicine, for the assessment of the working capacity of the employee, medical diagnosis, the provision of health or social care or treatment or the management of health or social care systems and services on the basis of EU or member state law or pursuant to contract with a health professional.

9   Processing is necessary for reasons of public interest in the area of public health, such as protecting against serious cross-border threats to health or ensuring high standards of quality and safety of health care and of medicinal products or medical devices, on the basis of EU or member state law.
10   Processing is necessary for archiving purposes in the public interest, scientific or historical research purposes or statistical purposes.

Processing of personal data relating to criminal convictions and offences or related security measures shall be carried out only under the control of official authority or when the processing is authorised by EU or member state law. Any comprehensive register of criminal convictions must be kept only under the control of official authority.

The Data Protection Act 2018 introduced new offences in order to comply with GDPR: for example, knowingly or recklessly obtaining or disclosing personal data without the consent of the data controller, procuring such disclosure, or retaining the data obtained without consent. Selling, or offering to sell, personal data knowingly or recklessly obtained or disclosed also became an offence.

Some definitions in UK data protection law

'Data' is broadly defined in Article 4 of the GDPR as information that is:

1   being processed by means of equipment operating automatically in response to instructions given for that purpose; or
2   recorded with the intention that it should be processed by means of such equipment; or
3   recorded as part of a relevant filing system or with the intention that it should form part of a relevant filing system; or
4   forms part of an accessible record (defined further below).

Information falling under any one of these headings constitutes 'data'. The first heading is simply computerised data. The term 'relevant filing system' is defined in Section 3 of the Data Protection Act 2018 as: 'any structured set of personal data which is accessible according to specific criteria, whether held by automated means or manually and whether centralised, decentralised or dispersed on a functional or geographical basis'.

Therefore, collections of papers in a folder that have no order or structure may be exempt from the Act. However, physical document collections with systematic ordering by a person's name or ID number are likely to fall within the remit of the Data Protection Act 2018.

The fourth heading ('accessible record') means certain health records created by a health professional, school records or a public record relevant to local authority housing or social services.

Only 'personal data' is subject to the Data Protection Act 2018. It is information relating to an identified, or identifiable, living individual. Data about corporations is not 'personal data'. An 'identified individual' is easy enough to understand. An 'identifiable individual' is someone who can be identified directly or indirectly from the information to hand. This could be by means of an ID number, by e-mail address or by some characteristic, associated with that individual. Thus the words 'the UK's Prime Minister' refer to an identifiable individual, and a recognisable photograph of a person, even if he or she is not named, may well be personal data. The Data Protection Act 2018 does not apply to data about dead people. The individual about whom data is held is known as the data subject. The data subject can be anybody in the world. As long as the data is under the control of a body that is UK-based, or is held in the UK, the Data Protection Act 2018 applies.

Data can be in any medium, and so includes microfilm, movie film, CCTV video, etc. – just so long as information or images of living identifiable individuals that can be readily retrieved by a search on the person's name or some form of ID, are involved.

Case study 2.3: Data protection structured filing systems

In October 2011, a then senior UK cabinet minister, Oliver Letwin, was caught disposing of letters sent to him from constituents into a waste bin in a park. In November 2011, confidential correspondence to another then senior minister, Vince Cable, was found outside his constituency offices. Some of the letters related to constituents' medical histories. On the face of it, this is sensitive personal data. However, the limitations of UK data protection law were highlighted because, although data in paper form is potentially covered by the Act, it has to be in a structured filing system before it is considered to be 'personal data'. Thus, a single letter, which has never been kept in a structured filing system, is exempt from the provisions of the Act.

It was noted above that some types of personal data are considered to be 'sensitive'. Perhaps surprisingly, financial information is *not* considered to be sensitive. Similarly, information about disciplinary proceedings against an individual, their exam or similar marks, or their DNA profile, is not sensitive personal data, but just falls under the heading of personal data. Sensitive personal data can be processed, but only under strictly controlled circumstances. Sensitive personal data that has been made public as a result of steps deliberately taken by the data subject may be processed. Sensitive personal data needed for legal proceedings, including prospective proceedings, for obtaining legal advice, to defend legal rights, for the administration of justice and for the exercise of statutory or government functions can also be processed. Processing sensitive personal data for ethnic monitoring, i.e. to check that an organisation is fulfilling its obligations under racial equality laws, is also permitted. Sensitive personal data can also be processed if the data controller obtains explicit written consent from the data subject. There is an implication here that the consequences of any consent have been fully explained to the data subject.

The data controller is any individual or undertaking that determines the purposes for which, and the manner in which, personal data is or will be processed. The data may be held in another country, but the organisation or individual that gives instructions regarding its use is the data controller. The ICO oversees the administration of data protection in the UK; its powers include:

◆ *handling requests for assessment* – any person can ask the ICO for an assessment of whether processing of data is being carried out in compliance with the Data Protection Act 2018

◆ *serving information notices* – the ICO may serve an 'information notice' on any data controller demanding information within a specified time from the controller

◆ *serving enforcement notices* – it may serve a notice requiring the data controller to amend, block, erase or destroy personal data

◆ *powers of entry* – it has the right to ask a judge or sheriff for a warrant to enter and search premises.

The ICO also has various duties to disseminate information, including guidance notes, and has the right to get the Crown Prosecution Service to initiate legal actions and/or can impose fines itself in cases of serious breaches of the Act.

The Data Protection Act 2018 imposes two relatively simple obligations on UK data controllers. The first is to notify the ICO of any processing of personal data that they carry out. The second is to abide by the data protection principles.

The rights of data subjects

Data subjects have, in essence, three rights under the Data Protection Act 2018. The first right is a right to find out about data held about them. Any data subject, wherever they live, has the right to be told if personal data is held about them upon written request. They are also entitled to see, in a form that is understandable, all personal data held about them by a controller. There can be no charge for responding in most cases.[2] Such requests are usually called subject access requests, or SARs.

The data controller has 30 days to respond to the SAR once it has received the request in writing. The data requested must be provided in 'permanent form'. This usually means a paper copy. However, but only if the data subject agrees to this, the data controller could pass the copy in, say, a memory stick. If supplying information to the data subject is likely to identify another individual, the controller is entitled to delete that part of the data relating to the other individual, unless that other individual has consented to this disclosure, or if it is not reasonable to delete the data.

The data subject is entitled to make as many SARs as they like, without cost, as often as they like, but a reasonable time must elapse between requests. Circumstances may arise where, when checking the data in response to a SAR, the data controller sees the data is inaccurate or misleading in some way. There may be a temptation to correct it before passing it to the data subject. The law states that such data may not be amended before being supplied, nor may it be deleted, unless it was going to be amended or deleted routinely anyway. It is, of course, an offence for a data controller to reply to a SAR with 'we don't hold any data on you' when in fact it knows it does.

---

2. https://ico.org.uk/for-organisations/guide-to-data-protection/guide-to-the-general-data-protection-regulation-gdpr/individual-rights/right-of-access

The data subject is also entitled to know if the data controller is processing data so as to make automated decisions about them. In such cases, the data subject is entitled to a description of the decision-making process, but there is no obligation to supply this in a form capable of being understood by the data subject!

The data subject is also entitled to prevent any processing that is causing, or is likely to cause 'unwarranted and substantial damage or distress' to either themselves or to others. In the case of direct marketing, the data subject need not even claim damage or distress. However, much unwanted marketing comes from countries outside the EU. The law offers little to help aggrieved data subjects regarding such unwanted marketing.

The data subject can ask a court to order correction, erasure or blocking of any data that is false or factually misleading.

Finally, the data subject is entitled to claim compensation for any breach of the Data Protection Act 2018 that has resulted in damage. Where there is quantifiable financial damage, further damages for distress can be demanded. Where the data have been processed for use by the media, claims can be for distress alone.

Exemptions under the law

Exemptions under the Data Protection Act 2018 vary according to the particular circumstances and nature of information and its use. This section only mentions a few. There are many others, and anyone advising others in their organisation needs to check the exemptions carefully.

Archiving purposes in the public interest [3]

Archiving in the public interest enables processing of personal data beyond the initial purpose and subsequent exemptions from some of the data protection obligations, which are attached to data subject rights. These include an exemption from the storage limitation principle, and an exemption from the right of erasure (the 'right to be forgotten').

---

3. See: www.nationalarchives.gov.uk/archives-sector/legislation/archives-data-protection-law-uk/gdpr-faqs

Journalism, literature, art

There are exemptions for publishing material containing personal information that falls in these special purposes. In this context, 'publishing' is defined as making available to the public or any section of the public, and so potentially includes social media postings. The following exemptions apply:

1   all the data protection principles except the seventh (it therefore remains important to maintain appropriate security arrangements against, for example, theft, loss or computer hacking)
2   data subject access rights
3   the data subject's right to prevent processing likely to cause damage or distress
4   the data subject's rights in relation to automated decision-taking
5   the data subject's rights to data rectification, blocking, erasure and destruction.

The exemption is designed to enable freedom of expression and the conduct of activity such as investigative journalism. The exemption is on a case-by-case basis, and is not a blanket exemption. It only applies to personal data being processed with a view to publication. The exemptions even extend to sensitive personal data, and so someone writing an article, say, about a politician's sex life benefits from the exemption. However, the exemption applies only to publication 'in the public interest'; presumably this would be decided on a case-by-case basis. Finally, the data controller must reasonably believe that compliance with the relevant provision of the Data Protection Act 2018 (e.g., a data subject's request to see what is held about him or her) is incompatible with freedom of expression. In other words, giving the individual access would prevent the publication of text that should be published in the public interest. The aggrieved individual is entitled to take the controller to court to get a judgment whether the exemption should apply or not. LIK workers may well be asked to give advice about this exemption to patrons who are doing journalistic work.

Research, including history and statistics

Researchers that use personal information enjoy certain exemptions, as long as the information is not processed:

◆ to support measures or decisions with respect to particular individuals; and

◆ in such a way that substantial damage or substantial distress is, or is likely to be, caused to any data subject.

LIK workers who undertake research themselves may well benefit from this exemption. Those who work in research-based organisations, such as universities or research and development-based industries, may well need to advise patrons who are undertaking research about this exemption.

Information available to the public by or under enactment

Information is often made available to the public as a requirement of legislation, e.g., the Register of Electors. Such information is exempt from certain of the Data Protection Act 2018 provisions. Again, LIK workers, particularly in public libraries, may well benefit from such an exemption or may be asked to advise about it.

Confidential references given by a data controller

The writer of a reference is not obliged to give the data subject access to its contents. The recipient of the reference, however, *is* obliged to show a data subject the references they have received, unless such a disclosure would breach someone else's privacy, e.g. the reference writer's, or someone else named in the reference. Of course, the reference writer's details can be redacted if need be. However, writers of references often are relaxed about providing a copy of the reference to the individual concerned.

Transfer of data out of the EEA

As noted earlier, it is a breach of the data protection law to transfer personal data outside the EEA unless the country to which the data has been transferred has what are considered to be adequate data protection laws; the person has consented to such a transfer; where the transfer is into a safe harbour or, for example, it is necessary for the implementation of a contractor; or it is legally required. 'Transfer' here means the deliberate sending of the data to the other country. As noted earlier, it does not include placing personal data on, say, a website so that someone in another country could download it. A good example of where personal data is transferred outside the EEA with the person's consent is Facebook.

Case study 2.4: Identifying personal data

The operators of a social networking space established to research and study interactions between users of the site with a view to developing the optimum environment want to keep records of the users of the site, but they are unsure as to what constitutes personal data within the meaning of the Data Protection Act 2018.

Personal data within the meaning of the Data Protection Act 2018 is data from which a living individual can be identified. Even if an individual is not immediately recognisable from a piece of datum, he/she may become identifiable by combining data in the possession of the data controller or which may come into the possession of the data controller. The key is as to whether the individual can be identified. Examples whether singly or collectively might include pictures, e-mail addresses, telephone numbers, place of work.

A reminder of the changes introduced by the GDPR

Increased territorial scope

The GDPR applies to all organisations processing personal data of data subjects residing in the EU, regardless of the processing organisation's location. The GPDR applies to the processing of personal data by controllers and processors in the EU, regardless of whether the processing takes place in the EU or not. The GDPR also applies to the processing of personal data of data subjects in the EU by a controller or processor not established in the EU, where the activities relate to: offering goods or services to EU citizens (irrespective of whether payment is required) and the monitoring of behaviour that takes place within the EU. Non-EU businesses processing the data of EU residents will also have to appoint a representative in the EU.

Penalties

Organisations in breach of GDPR can be fined up to 4% of annual global turnover or €20 million (whichever is greater). This is the maximum fine that can be imposed for the most serious infringements, e.g., not having consent to process data. There is a tiered approach to fines, e.g. a company can be fined 2% for not having their records in order, not notifying the supervising authority and data subject about a breach or not conducting an impact assessment. It is important to note that these rules apply to both controllers and processors. It is worth noting that the ICO has stated that it has no plans to significantly increase the level of fines it imposes for breaches in the UK to the maximum level allowed for under GDPR.

Consent

The conditions for consent have been strengthened, as the request for it must be given in an intelligible and easily accessible form, with the purpose for data processing supplied. It must be as easy to withdraw consent as it is to give it.

Breach notification

Notification is mandatory where a data breach is likely to 'result in a risk for the rights and freedoms of individuals'. This must be done within 72 hours of first having become aware of the breach. Data processors will also be required to notify their customers and the controllers, 'without undue delay' after first becoming aware of a data breach. Breaches could include e-mails/data/letters sent to the wrong people, putting personal data on social media, or information left on laptops or memory sticks left in plain view or stolen. Arguably even having a loud conversation on a mobile phone in a public place, such as a train, in which personal data is mentioned, could be a breach. We don't necessarily recommend that someone goes over to the culprit and say to them 'you do realise you are breaking the Data Protection Act, don't you?', but in principle this could be done. Data breaches also include inappropriate alteration, loss or destruction of personal data.

Personal data breaches can include:

◆   access by an unauthorised third party through their direct action or lax internal security procedures or practices
◆   deliberate or accidental action or inaction by a member of staff

◆ sending personal data to an incorrect recipient, e.g. wrong recipients to an e-mail
◆ USB stick, laptop or phone containing personal data being lost or stolen
◆ alteration of personal data without permission
◆ loss of availability of personal data.

When a security incident takes place, it must be established whether a personal data breach has occurred, the nature of that breach, and the steps that need to be taken in response to the breach. If a breach is not addressed promptly and with the appropriate sense of urgency, then more damage may result. For this reason, there are tight deadlines for reporting and action. A notifiable breach (i.e. a breach that is a risk to the rights and freedoms of individuals) must be reported to the ICO without undue delay, and not later than 72 hours after becoming aware of it. Where this time deadline is not met, then reasons for the delay must be explained.

Right to access

The right for data subjects to obtain from the data controller confirmation as to whether or not personal data concerning them is being processed, where and for what purpose, is confirmed. Further, the controller has to provide a copy of the personal data, free of charge, in an electronic format if this is acceptable to the requester. If made available in machine-readable form, the data should be in a standard readable format, such as a Microsoft Word document. Charges can only be made for repeated requests.

Fees and registration

Organisations no longer have to fill out a long form to register with the ICO. There are four different fee levels, from free of charge to £2900. The fee level depends on staff numbers, annual turnover, the type of organisation, and the sorts of personal data handled. The maximum fee is for large organisations.[4] Fees have to be paid annually, and there are fines imposed for failure to pay. There is no fee payable if the individual or organisation is only using the data for one or more of the following reasons:

---

4. See https://ico.org.uk/for-organisations/guide-to-data-protection/guide-to-the-general-data-protection-regulation-gdpr/data-protection-fee

◆ staff administration
◆ advertising, marketing and public relations
◆ accounts and records
◆ not-for-profit purposes
◆ personal, family or household affairs
◆ maintaining a public register
◆ judicial functions
◆ processing personal information without an automated system
◆ if the individual using the data is an MP, or a prospective MP. However, staff employed by such individuals are not exempt from paying a fee.

For all others, the minimum annual fee is £40.

Right to be forgotten

This entitles the data subject to have the data controller 'erase' their personal data, cease further dissemination of the data, and potentially have third parties halt processing of the data. 'Erase' in this context means access to the data is blocked, rather than necessarily having the data completely removed. The conditions for erasure include the data no longer being relevant to original purposes for processing, or the data subject withdrawing consent. It should also be noted that this right requires controllers to balance the subjects' rights with 'the public interest in the availability of the data' when considering such requests.

Data portability

This is the right for a data subject to receive the personal data concerning them, which they have previously provided, in a commonly used machine-readable format (presumably in MS Word, PDF, as a csv file or similar) and have the right to transmit that data to another controller.

Privacy by design

This is now a legal requirement. It calls for the inclusion of data protection from the start of the design of systems. Specifically, the controller should implement appropriate technical and organisational measures to protect the rights of data subjects. It calls for controllers to hold and process only the data absolutely necessary for the completion of its duties as well as limiting the access to personal data to those needing to access it or to carry out processing of the personal data.

Data protection officers

Data protection officers (DPOs):

◆ must be appointed on the basis of professional qualities and, in particular, expert knowledge on data protection law and practice[5]
◆ can be a member of staff, or an external service provider[6]
◆ their contact details must be provided to the relevant data protection authority, i.e., the ICO in the UK
◆ must be provided with appropriate resources to carry out their tasks and maintain their expert knowledge
◆ are required for all public bodies (such as those subject to FoI – see Chapter 3), or any other organisation if it regularly and systematically monitors data subjects, or if it processes a large amount of sensitive personal data
◆ must report directly to the highest level of management
◆ must not carry out any other tasks or have a line manager that could result in a conflict of interest, e.g., reporting to the IT Manager.

The role of the DPO within organisations is further discussed in Chapter 8.

Derogations

The GDPR gives EU member states the ability to derogate or amend the law on matters relating to national security, the law, defence, public security, anything to do with criminal offences, and important public interests. Whilst the GDPR encourages the idea that an association can take up the cause of multiple individuals in a complaint, the UK implementation restricts the making of complaints to those individuals that have been affected.

---

5. This could include, of course, attending relevant courses and obtaining relevant certificates or qualifications.
6. No doubt some individuals or organisations will offer their services as data protection officers to multiple third parties.

Top tips

1   Data protection compliance is an ongoing process of compliance. It did not begin and end with GDPR.
2   Data protection issues will affect all types of carriers of personal data – not just digital. This will include paper records, photographs, sound recordings, films, etc. It's unlikely one system can manage all GDPR issues but instead, a series of compliance interventions will be required.
3   Good privacy management is a positive step for demonstrating trust and good practice. This is certainly good for business and building trusted relationships with third parties.
4   Not all data breaches need to be declared to the ICO, but it is vital that, no matter what, an organisation has sensible data breach policies in place to record any that happen. Breaches that have to be declared to the ICO include any loss or theft of personal data that could potentially cause harm or distress to the individual concerned.

Further reading

Denley, A., Foulsham, M. and Hitchen, B. (2019) *GDPR: how to achieve and maintain compliance*, Routledge.

Voigt, P. and von dem Bussche, A. (2017) *The EU GDPR: a practical guide*, Springer.

 **Freedom of information**

Introduction

Freedom of information (FoI) is legislation that obliges government and other public bodies to reveal documents, data collections, etc., to any members of the public, including the media. Many countries around the world have FoI laws, including the UK. The relevant legislation in England and Wales is the Freedom of Information Act 2000, which also covers Northern Ireland at the moment. Scotland has its own Freedom of Information (Scotland) Act 2002.

The following organisations, many of which employ LIK staff, are covered by UK FoI legislation:

◆ government departments
◆ local councils
◆ schools, colleges and universities
◆ health trusts, hospitals and doctors' surgeries
◆ publicly funded museums
◆ the police
◆ non-departmental public bodies, committees and advisory bodies
◆ BBC and Channel 4.

The House of Commons and the Independent Parliamentary Standards Authority are both subject to FoI, but individual Members of Parliament are not.

This means that LIK workers working in such organisations need to understand the circumstances in which they may be asked for, and subsequently may (or may not) need to supply, information to third parties. Furthermore, professionals working in sectors not subject to FoI also need to be aware of the possibilities offered by FoI to help answer queries posed by their patrons.

UK FoI legislation includes a particularly long list of exemptions compared with the legislation in other countries. Unlike data protection, the UK's FoI laws are not tied to any EU Directive or Regulation.[1] There is separate legislation in respect of information of relevance to the environment (the Environmental Information Regulations 2004, SI2004/and similar Scots legislation), but that is not considered further in this chapter.

In the EU, many individual member states have explicit FoI laws, or FoI is written into the country's constitution. In addition, a EU Regulation provides FoI for the three main EU institutions to EU citizens and natural or legal persons residing, or with registered offices in, a member state (Regulation (EC) No 1049/2001 of the European Parliament and the Council of 30 May 2001 regarding public access to European Parliament, Council and Commission documents). For most other EU bodies and agencies, there is a provision in the legal act establishing them which makes Regulation No 1049/2001 applicable to them as well. Directive 2003/98/EC of the European Parliament and the Council of 17 November 2003 on the reuse of public sector information (updated in 2013) sets out the rules and practices for accessing public sector information resources for further exploitation. Finally, Directive 2003/4/EC provides for citizens of each country to have freedom of access to information on the environment, in line with the requirements of the Aarhus Convention.[2] Governments are required to transcribe the directive into national legislation.

A basic purpose of FoI legislation is to increase transparency, and thereby reduce the public's distrust of government. The rationale for FoI is that it gives the public greater access to the workings of government, and a better-informed electorate ensures better government. It reduces the need for whistle-blowing and leaks, and helps reduce the chances that governments make expensive mistakes or corrupt decisions. In the UK, FoI

---

1. As noted in the last chapter, an EU Regulation requires member states to implement legislation pretty much word for word as presented in it; a Directive, in contrast, gives the member state much more flexibility in interpretation and implementation. Confusingly, in UK law, a 'Regulation' is a piece of secondary legislation (a Statutory Instrument), which is an amendment to some primary legislation (an Act of Parliament).
2. See https://en.wikipedia.org/wiki/Aarhus_Convention

legislation was only passed with great reluctance by the then Labour government, and the Prime Minister Tony Blair is on record as saying that the legislation was the worst mistake he made, a remark that would be viewed with surprise by many. As already noted, the UK's Act has many exemptions, which make it less useful than the laws in other countries. Thus, for example, it was only after many struggles over the applicability of the Act that the campaigner Heather Brooke finally uncovered a scandal regarding UK Parliamentary expenses. This case set a precedent that government cannot refuse to disclose details about a public sector employee's salary band and/or expenses.

There is tension between FoI and data protection, as the latter is designed to prevent the unauthorised disclosure of information about individuals, whilst the former tries to expose as much as possible. Thus, for example, whilst arguably information about the health of the Prime Minister is of value to the public when assessing the actions of the government, such revelations could be a breach of data protection law. The law resolves this by ensuring that data protection trumps FoI if there is such a conflict and if disclosure would be 'unwarranted'. Of course, that leaves open to debate what is, or is not, unwarranted. Data protection law addresses this tension to some extent by giving an individual under some circumstances the right to request modification and/or erasure of information held about them.

Incidentally, there is separate legislation (The Re-use of Public Sector Information Regulations 2015) that requires many government bodies to hand over, for a fee that reflects the cost of reproduction only, data or information to anyone who requires it for their own commercial exploitation purposes. The idea behind this is to encourage entrepreneurs to make use of valuable information if they can, as a result, generate income from it and thereby improve economic conditions. The entrepreneur does not have to be UK-based. Thus, for example, census data that is available could be copied and used by a service offering genealogical research. This legislation is not discussed further in this chapter. FoI legislation is also unrelated to the public's access to records held by the Public Record Office; that is covered by the Public Records Act 1958, and related legislation for parts of the UK outside England and Wales, and is not discussed further in this book.

Some details of the UK law

The law in the UK[3] gives any person the right to know if a public authority holds certain information, and to obtain copies of said information. The person or organisation making the request can be anyone anywhere in the world. No questions should be asked about their motives for asking. The requester can use a pseudonym if required, but if he or she does, then they have no right of appeal against a refusal to supply the information. The Freedom of Information Act 2000 has an associated Code of Practice (discussed in Chapter 8). Whilst there is no legal obligation to follow this Code, in practice, most bodies do.

The Freedom of Information Act 2000 refers to 'information', and defines this term as 'information recorded in any form'. This is not as silly a definition as one might first think, because of the word *recorded*. This means the information must exist in material form, e.g., be in print, handwriting, audio, video, or of course in any digital form. The information in question may form part or all of a single item, or might be scattered amongst many recorded items. If the information happens to include references to a living identifiable person and disclosure might breach data protection law, the responding public body is entitled to remove such personal details before handing it over. If on the other hand, the document is solely about an individual, then there may well be grounds to refuse the requester permission to view a copy of the item.

The information has, of course, to be held by one of the bodies subject to FoI law as listed above, or by someone acting on behalf of them. It does not have to be physically in the UK, as long as the authority is based in the UK. Information that has been, or is about to be, routinely deleted, does not have to be copied and supplied to the requester. In theory, the law is very tough on anyone who, having received a FoI request, chooses to deny it, holds the information, or deletes the information rather than copy and supply it, but in practice it can be very difficult to prove that such an action was as a result of a FoI request. If, of course, the material is held in electronic form, backup files should be checked as well as the current one.

There is a long list of organisations under the Freedom of Information Act 2000 deemed to be public authorities or bodies, and therefore subject to FoI (Schedule 1 of the Freedom of Information Act 2000). As noted

---

3. Unless otherwise identified, this chapter discusses the Freedom of Information Act 2000, as Scottish legislation is similar in most regards

earlier, they include government departments, Parliament, the armed forces, local government bodies, fire authorities, the National Health Service, schools, colleges, universities, the British Council, police forces, HM Revenue and Customs, etc. Also as noted above, in some cases, the BBC and Channel 4 are subject to the Act, as are nationalised organisations. Certain private companies that carry out public services, such as those running prisons and detention centres and refuse collection, are also subject to FoI. It should be noted that private sector organisations that supply public library services are subject to FoI. Water, gas and electricity companies are subject to the Environmental Information Regulations.[4] Some bodies, such as the Secret Service and GCHQ, are not subject to FoI, and indeed, many queries that might be passed to the police will be refused; the grounds for exemption from FoI are considered below. Certain libraries and information departments are likely to find themselves the subject of FoI requests. These include university, NHS, public, school, government and national libraries, as well as national archives. In addition, of course, LIK staff in any organisation might be asked to assist a patron who wants to use FoI.

In addition to the obligation to supply information, all public authorities are obliged to develop and publish (typically on the web) a 'publication scheme'. These link to documents made available to the public by the organisation. One side effect is the need for a member of staff to create and maintain such publication schemes; often these are LIK workers. Many organisations employ full-time or part-time staff to handle incoming FoI requests, and these are sometimes LIK workers.

All FoI requests should be made in writing (which can include e-mail). There is no obligation to respond to oral requests, e.g., by phone, though many bodies choose to do so. The requester must give their name (or pseudonym) and contact address – which could be an e-mail address. As full a description as possible of the required information should be provided. There is no obligation to use the phrase 'freedom of information', and so staff need to be trained to recognise that a request for information might fall under the legislation and therefore must be complied with. The public authority is obliged to assist if the requester has difficulty expressing their request – or should recommend where the requester should go to help formulate their request properly. It is not clear what obligations rest

---

4. As noted above, in UK law, Regulations are secondary legislation and not an EU instruction.

on the public authority if the request is made by someone who is not a native English speaker, but we recommend that a reasonable amount of help is provided to the requester.

The public authority is entitled to charge a reasonable fee reflecting the cost of extracting and supplying the requested information, and whilst many do, some do not. The information must be supplied within a maximum of 20 working days from receipt of the request, or of the fee, whichever is the later. In some exceptional circumstances, the length of time can be extended. Failure to fulfil a request within the time limit can lead to problems if the requester makes a complaint to the Information Commissioner.[5] The maximum fee for long and complex requests can be high, or, if the amount of work required is considered excessive, the authority can decline to fulfil the request. However, in such cases, the authority is obliged to inform the requester and advise on how to make the request more manageable. Photocopying costs can be added to the fee where appropriate. Proposed fees can be challenged by the requester by going to the Information Commissioner to make a complaint. Material given to the requester must be a permanent copy, e.g., on paper, on a memory stick, etc., as the requester prefers. Alternatively, the applicant can be invited to the authority's premises to inspect the material, or can just obtain a summary, but the choice is the requester's. The authority can refuse a request it considers vexatious (e.g., from someone who simply wants to cause problems to the authority by asking for large amounts of information every few days, or repeating the same request week after week for no good reason) or excessive. Not all public authorities are as diligent as they should be in replying to requests on time, or for giving good reasons why the information cannot be supplied.[6]

Although the requester is entitled to receive the information requested in permanent form, that does not necessarily give them the right to further reproduce it. This is because it may well be in copyright, either belonging to the public authority or some third party. However, an Information

---

5. The Information Commissioner's Office (ICO) is responsible for good practice regarding both FoI and DP in the UK. Its website can be found at www.ico.org.uk. This includes helpful guides to the use of FoI, e.g. https://ico.org.uk/for-organisations/guide-to-freedom-of-information is for organisations receiving FoI requests.
6. The website www.foiman.com is good for keeping an eye on such issues. Another website, www.whatdotheyknow.com, is useful for tracking the types of FoI requests that have been made in the past.

Commissioner's decision declared that it is *not* unlawful to place the requested materials on a website.[7] Of course, the information may not be in the form of a literary work, but might be a database, which may or may not be protected by copyright and/or database right (see Chapter 1 for more on this).

Exemptions to FoI

The most controversial area of the UK's FoI laws is the long list of exemptions (Freedom of Information Act 2000, pt 2), whereby a public authority has grounds for refusing to disclose the information requested. There are two types of exemption – absolute (which require no explanation) and qualified (where the authority has to justify why it is refusing to supply the information). Absolute exemptions include the following:

◆ The information is already reasonably available elsewhere (though this exemption raises questions where the information is available elsewhere but it is difficult or expensive to access; the reasonableness test is important). This is an exemption libraries are quite likely to use in response to FoI requests, or indeed libraries may find patrons making requests to view particular materials in their library because a public authority has recommended to a requester that this is the place to go for the information.

◆ The information relates to an ongoing programme of research and there is an intention by someone to publish a report of the research, and disclosure of the information would or would be likely to prejudice the research programme, the interests of participants in the programme, or a public authority holding or intending to publish a report of the research. There does not have to be any intention to publish the particular information that has been requested, nor does there need to be an identified publication date. Libraries, too, may well use this exemption.

◆ The information relates to national security, the armed forces, or international relations.

---

7. The ICO provides some guidance on this issue at https://ico.org.uk/media/for-organisations/documents/1150/intellectual_property_rights_and_disclosures_under_the_foia.pdf.

◆ The information relates to the administration of justice.
◆ The information would breach Parliamentary privilege (but this exemption failed in the case of MPs' expenses, and so perhaps should not be considered an absolute exemption).
◆ This is personal information and cannot be reproduced because of data protection law.
◆ This is information which if revealed would lead to an action for breach of confidence (simply marking something as 'confidential' is not enough to enjoy this exemption).
◆ Disclosure would be a breach of the law, e.g., contempt of court, defamatory, etc.

The applicant is entitled to appeal to the ICO if they do not like the decision, and indeed, can further appeal against an ICO decision if need be.

There is also a long list of qualified exemptions, where the authority has to apply a public interest test, i.e. what is more important, keeping the information confidential or releasing it? The public authority makes the decision, but again, the applicant can appeal against such a decision. Amongst these qualified exemptions are the following:

◆ information intended for future publication (it must be genuinely intended, not just vaguely planned); a library might use in response to a request for information on usage figures
◆ information relating to defence matters
◆ information relating to international relations, or relations between the government and the devolved administrations of Wales, Northern Ireland and Scotland
◆ criminal investigations and proceedings
◆ the auditing of public bodies; a publicly funded library may well use this exemption
◆ formulation of government policy – a very broad exemption that is often used, and could be applicable to government libraries that receive a FoI request
◆ information relating to the country's economic performance
◆ information that could affect people's health and safety; an NHS library might have to use this exemption from time to time
◆ information that would prejudice the conduct of public affairs – a very broad exemption

◆ information relating to legal professional privilege
◆ trade secrets or any information that is likely to prejudice the commercial interests of any person or organisation; there are a number of scenarios where this might apply to a library, e.g. a request for information on the costs of certain library subscriptions, or to view the terms of a contract that the library has entered into
◆ information relating to the royal family
◆ information relating to the honours system.

This is a much longer list of exemptions than in most other countries with FoI legislation, and some of these headings are so broad as to apparently defeat the whole object of FoI. Although the requester can appeal to the ICO against a decision its powers, as we shall see, are somewhat limited.

Case study 3.1: The Matrix Report

In December 2014, a journalist approached the Department of Business, Innovation and Skills (a UK government department, hereinafter 'BIS') to request the following information under the Freedom of Information Act:

Early in 2014, the research company Matrix was commissioned to prepare a report for BIS into open access to research outputs. An economist employed at BIS commissioned the report. I would be grateful if you could provide a copy of the commissioning/scope document outlining exactly what BIS wanted Matrix to do, a copy of the report itself, plus copies of all letters, e-mails, meeting and phone notes, and any recordings connected with the report and discussions about it.

In January 2015, BIS replied that the Department had not yet reached a decision on this FoI request regarding the balance of the public interest with respect to information intended for future publication, or possibly other exemptions under the FoI Act. Then in February 2015, it wrote again to the journalist informing him that other than a few details, such as the total funds given to Matrix, it would not be releasing any further information in view of the intention to publish the Matrix Report. The letter also informed the journalist that the report had been due to be published during 2014, but had been delayed because of 'the complexity of some of the methodological issues involved.' The letter, however, stated that publication of the report would occur some time in 2015, and it would therefore not be in the public interest to disclose the report or background to it until the report had been published. It also stated that it could not provide the information requested at that time as it might affect the formulation of Government policy – another exemption in the Freedom of Information Act 2000.

If the BIS genuinely planned to publish the Matrix Report, it was indeed entitled not to pass a copy of that report in advance of publication, whether or not a publication date had been set.

As noted in this chapter, the UK's 'formulation of government policy' exemption is a convenient method for avoiding FoI obligations. Many other countries' FoI laws do not include it, but it's there in UK law.

At the time this chapter was drafted (November 2019), the Matrix Report had not been published. This case study demonstrates the way that government and other bodies subject to FoI can evade their responsibilities under FoI by use of a choice of wide-ranging exemptions.

The Information Commissioner's Office (ICO)

In many countries, there are two separate bodies responsible for overseeing the administration of information-related laws, i.e. one for FoI and one for data protection. In the UK, both sets of responsibility lie with the ICO.[8] The ICO can demand details of responses from public authorities and can issue orders following an investigation after a complaint has been received from a requester. It can also impose penalties on authorities that break the law. As with data protection, it also has the right to inspect premises and, if need be, get a warrant to enter premises.

There is an Information Tribunal, which can hear appeals against the ICO's decision on anything to do with either FoI or data protection. However, the government can ignore a ruling relating to FoI from either the ICO, or from the Tribunal. Thus, ultimately, the ICO cannot impose its will on a government that refuses to follow an ICO decision on an FoI matter. There are other problems with the ICO's role, too. It does not have enough staff to investigate all the complaints it receives, and this, combined with the wide exemptions granted under FoI legislation makes the law far less useful than it might seem at first glance.

---

8. Scotland has its own Information Commissioner for FoI and environmental information matters only.

The overlap between FoI and data protection

As has already been noted, there is a tension between FoI and SARs (subject access requests), which readers need to be aware of. This is particularly important, as requests for information do not have to use the words 'data protection', 'subject access request' or 'freedom of information' to be legally valid requests. Anyone receiving a request for information should consider the following questions:

For possible FoI requests

1 Is my organisation one of those that fall within the remit of FoI?
2 If 'yes', is this request for information a potentially valid one under FoI?
3 If 'yes', do any of the exemptions allowed for under FoI apply to this request? If so, is/are the exemption(s) absolute or qualified?
4 If an appropriate exemption is applicable you can – assuming the public interest test does not override any qualified exemption – decline the request, giving a full explanation to the requester for the reasons within the time allowed; if 'no', you should organise the supply of the information requested. If the problem is that the information requested includes personal data about third parties, you still may have to supply the information, but with information about the individuals redacted. Consultation with the data protection expert in the organisation (if it is someone different) is necessary if personal data is likely to be disclosed.

For possible SARs

1 Is this, whether worded as such or not, an SAR?
2 If yes, has the person identified himself or herself to your satisfaction (you are entitled to demand proof of identity, such as copy of passport, recent bank statements, etc.)?
3 Do any of the exemptions apply to this request? If so, reply to the requester giving a full explanation of the reasons for refusal. Of course, one reason for refusal could be simply that no information about the individual is held. If the problem is that the information requested includes personal data about third parties, you still may be

required to supply the information, but with information about the third parties redacted.

4 Is this one of the (rare) cases where we are entitled to charge the requester?

Top tips

1 LIK workers need to understand the circumstances in which they may be asked for information, how they should respond, when they need to supply the requested information and when they don't have to.

2 Staff need to be aware that FoI requests should be responded to within 20 working days of the original request.

3 Staff should be made aware of their FoI obligations through training and supported through the use of relevant tools and templates – see Chapters 9 and 10 of this book.

4 SARs are not the same as FoI requests. Any organisation that is publicly funded and subject to FoI must ensure that suitable procedures are in place to distinguish between the two, and to recognise when a FoI request might have data protection implications. The procedures should include an identity verification process for SARs to prevent personal data being sent to the wrong person, thereby creating a breach of the Data Protection Act 2018.

Further reading

Gibbons, P. (2019) *The Freedom of Information Officer's Handbook*, Facet Publishing.

4 Governance, audits and risk assessment

Introduction

Management of information should be a strategic concern in all organisations. They need information to function effectively and for decision-making. Increasingly, information has been recognised as an asset to be exploited as, for example, in intellectual property. This was first publicised in the KPMG report *Information as an Asset: the board agenda* (Hawley, 1995), confirmed through research (for example see Oppenheim, Stenson and Wilson, 2002) and revived in 2019 through CILIP.[1]

Information law compliance takes place within broader information governance frameworks. Information governance refers to control of the use of information throughout its lifecycle from creation to preservation or destruction. The goal of information governance is to ensure the following:

◆ identification of information assets, their quality and their value to the organisation
◆ that the information is secure and is available and accessible however and whenever it is required and, at the same time, no unauthorised person can access it
◆ development, communication and implementation of policies and procedures for information management that address organisational

---

1. At the time this book was written, the UK was still a member of the European Union and ECJ decisions applied to it. If the UK does leave the EU, future ECJ decisions will not automatically apply in the UK, though in practice, we expect UK courts will often still follow the decisions taken by the ECJ.

goals, comply with all legal and regulatory frameworks and are responsive to change

◆ people within the organisation have the necessary knowledge, skills and authority to be aware of, and implement, appropriate policies and procedures.

Information governance frameworks

Information governance frameworks are concerned with the management of information in all its forms, information systems and information security, within the organisation. The scope of information governance frameworks also encompasses legal, regulatory and any external information that has an impact on the organisation's obligations. All staff involved in the creation, management, use and sharing of information should be covered by these frameworks, which set out policies and procedures and the rights and roles of staff, suppliers, users, customers and all other stakeholders.

Information governance frameworks should include a range of policies, recognising all aspects of information management and use. Such policies should include information, records and archives management; information systems and security; compliance with information-related laws, such as data protection, and copyright; and information sharing, including FoI in the case of public bodies. Staff training and development policies are also crucial to ensure policies are implemented correctly. The business case for information legal compliance policies is not hard to make. The benefits include reducing the risks of copyright infringements, failure to abide by FoI requirements and data breaches, each of which can lead to consequential reputational damage. Policies can also promote efficiency savings, by providing the framework for more streamlined processes and avoidance of duplication of procedures as well as good data and information hygiene practices. Such a set of policies should guide the creation of transparent and clear parameters for staff by establishing roles and responsibilities. Intellectual property (IP) policies can both prevent haemorrhaging of IP assets as well as opportunities for the exploitation of IP assets for the organisation's benefit. There will also be the added benefit of professionalising the external offer of an organisation to its funders, partners, suppliers, clients, contractors, students (in the case of educational establishments) and other third parties.

Roles in information governance

Owning and implementing organisation-wide legal compliance is everyone's responsibility, but ultimately, it must be driven from the top. In an environment where staff are supported by strong leadership and good management, a robust and compliant information management culture is easier to achieve and less likely to be derailed by obstacles such as an unwillingness by staff to engage along the way. Legal compliance is not always easy nor clear-cut, so establishing a governance framework accepts that there may be risks and difficult decisions, but the appropriate structure is in place to support the organisation and its staff in coming to those decisions. There will also be circumstances where the governance rules are not solely driven by the law, but also by what is considered to be good professional practice.

Moreover, accepting that rights and privacy compliance continually require review, investment and consideration, will ensure that changes in organisational structures and/or technology, new staff, changes to the law, project and activity developments are supported by a 'rights and privacy by design' culture whereby copyright and privacy rights are built into organisational culture through the integration of these considerations across all information and data touch points. In such a culture, staff feel safe and supported to make decisions on behalf of their organisation and to be able to push issues of concern up to senior management. Senior management, in turn, take responsibility for any high-level risks, deciding whether the risk is too high for the organisation or not. They are then empowering staff to feel safe not only in expressing concerns to them, but also to challenge others if they identify areas of risk. Moreover, it sends clear messages to other staff in the organisation that these staff are not just being obstructive; rather, they are acting as agents of help within their organisation.

Indeed, supported staff with versatile skills and proficiencies will be able to better monitor other staff, negotiate with rights holders, consider how rights and permissions can be managed more efficiently and ensure that appropriate organisational tools, procedures and policies are in place to ensure compliance with legal requirements relating to data and information. They will be able to recognise when risks might be suitable to take, and how these risks can be mitigated (risk management is discussed later in this chapter). They can act as gatekeepers to better practices, support fellow staff and other stakeholders better and help move the organisation from risk-averse to risk-aware.

Governance committees or boards

Senior staff across the organisation should lead on information governance, including senior LIK and records managers. Governance committees[2] (also known as governance boards) should include staff from all parts of the organisation that are directly involved or affected, such as legal and compliance managers, chief information officers, records, data quality, service and security managers as well as human resources managers, ensuring a holistic approach. Of course, the level of seniority of members of the group, and the number of people involved, will depend on the type and size of organisation. Geographical issues will also be relevant; it is obviously easier to set up such a committee if the organisation is based in one location, but video conferencing and other related technologies can be used for the successful creation and running of such a committee even in an organisation operating in widely dispersed locations.

The terms of reference of the information governance committee should be clearly set out. These will include committee remit, authority and accountability; membership (including who is the chair of the committee), member roles and reporting; frequency of meetings, agenda-setting and the taking of minutes. Examples of terms of reference documents are available online,[3] particularly for health-related services. The remit of the governance committee is usually to take a strategic approach to information governance and oversee the development and implementation of policy and procedures to achieve strategic objectives, including the monitoring of performance against these objectives. Part of the committee's remit will be to maintain an overview of statutory requirements and arrangements for information law compliance. As well as monitoring implementation of policies and plans, such governance committees will also receive reports of any adverse incidents such as data breaches or other legal infringements, as well as reports of FoI requests and SARs, and take

---

2. Of course, individuals or very small organisations will not need such a formal approach.
3. For example: a London NHS trust, www.candi.nhs.uk/sites/default/files/Documents/
Board%20papers/03.12%20BoD%20%28Public%29%2030.07.15%20-%20Appendix%202%20-
%20ToR%20Information%20Committee%20-January%202015.pdf; an English university,
www.liverpool.ac.uk/governance/university-committees/informationgovernancecommittee

decisions on actions to be taken. The committee may, of course, decide that it needs internal or external consultants to carry out information audits and/or review the organisation's information management policies and to make recommendations for any necessary changes.

Senior Responsible Officer

An information governance manager, sometimes called the Senior Responsible Officer in large public sector organisations, takes ownership and is accountable for delivery of the information governance programme across the organisation. This is an important role and, in some cases, the information governance manager may lead a team tasked with practical implementation of governance frameworks. The focus at this level will be co-ordination, enforcement, monitoring and review of alignment between strategic objectives, policies and procedures. Amongst the responsibilities of the governance manager will be management of risk and dealing with serious problems. The first tasks in information risk management should be to develop information audit and risk management processes and procedures, and/or to review current policies and procedures.

Organisations, including their LIK services, need to know what information they have, why they have it, what form(s) it is in, when it was created, whether it is due for updating, and where and how it is stored. The number and nature of backups and disaster planning scenarios will also need to be addressed. They need to be clear about how information can be used lawfully, who should have access to it and which parts can and should be shared internally and externally. Audits will also expose what the organisation does not know about its information, for example, records of who owns the rights in information or other types of intellectual property held by the organisation, or the legal bases for recording and processing personal data. These activities require the involvement of the managers of each organisational function, as they are the individuals who will be best placed to understand the risks that apply to their part of the organisation and how best to mitigate those risks. The outputs from audits and risk assessments should inform the development of risk policies and procedures for implementing and monitoring compliance with these policies. At the end of this process, the organisation will be much more risk aware, but it is important to note that it is likely that a cost/benefit analysis will have to be made in respect of recommended actions, and the organisation will have to decide its tolerance levels for risk. Tolerance levels may differ depending on the nature of the risk and the organisation's information policies will reflect these differing tolerance levels. The focus will probably be on the impact of risks, including financial loss, legal liability and reputational damage.

Compliance officers

Other roles in information law compliance include data protection officers (DPOs) and FoI officers (these roles are often combined in public authorities), copyright officers and departmental information governance champions who can support their department's specific compliance requirements and feed back to the copyright/DPO/FoI officer and/or governance committee as required. As discussed in Chapter 2, the GDPR requires a strategic role for the DPO for many organisations. This is certainly the case for public bodies or authorities. We also noted in Chapter 2 that information professionals can play roles in FoI compliance through the development of publication schedules, implementation of records and information management standards and good practice. In organisations where information is considered an asset, information asset managers will be involved in audits and creating asset registers. Information asset managers will record designated asset owners and be involved in developing policies and procedures for information asset management. Records managers will have a similar role in the development and management of policy and procedures for the classification, retention, archiving and disposal of records. LIK services may have their own copyright officers to support staff and users in making lawful use of copyright works.

Case study 4.1: The role of the information governance committee/board

An information governance board was established in a publicly funded organisation, to implement and monitor the effectiveness of GDPR compliance across the organisation. The archivist, who was leading on GDPR implementation, used the governance board to report back on successes, as well as ensure that members both fed into the process of implementation and were able to feed back from their teams about issues and concerns. The governance board was chaired by one of the organisation's directors, who regularly reported back to other members of the senior leadership team.

Audits

It is impossible to implement a successful information strategy, including factors such as what information is needed, what information can be licensed in, information that is licensable out, and compliance with statutory requirements such as data protection or copyright, without knowing the information (including data, records and intellectual property) that is owned and/or held by your organisation and the rights in this information. Information professionals are likely to be both at the forefront of giving advice to others within their organisation regarding information law matters, but also in collecting the necessary data to understand fully what information or data is held by the organisation, and what needs to be held by it. It is indeed possible that members of LIK staff will be the ones who carry out the entire legal compliance audit process. The information in question might be in digital or analogue form; it may be textual, numeric, contain images (still or moving), or include sound recordings or performances. It probably will be derived from multiple sources. Some of the material may well qualify as 'orphan works' (see Chapter 1).

In this chapter, we recommend the steps that should be taken to carry out an information audit with a view to legal compliance. This is separate from, though will overlap with, an information asset audit such as that recommended by Burk and Horton (1988). The purpose of the information audit is to ensure that the information and records that the organisation processes are managed in accordance with best-practice procedures and comply with legislation and regulation. The audit is a risk mitigation exercise and quality improvement process. By understanding what information the organisation holds and how this is being processed, it can assess where there are areas of risk and put procedures in place for improving the management of information.

The benefits of carrying out a legal compliance information audit include the following:

◆   identification of potential rights issues which may exist in content

- identification of different types of rights present in any one item, or a collection of items
- the calculation of the duration of rights associated with any given item or collection of items
- identification of items where the rights might be owned by third parties
- identification of all relevant rights holders, with contact details
- identification of terms and conditions for licensing in information owned by third parties
- identification of any information that is subject to data protection legislation, and therefore must be handled in accordance with that legislation, and which might also be liable to be covered by an SAR (see Chapter 2)
- identification of information that may be the subject of a FoI request (see Chapter 3)
- identification of items that might be orphan works
- identification of rights that belong to the organisation, and which need to be protected and/or exploited
- development of a risk management strategy to ensure that the information within the organisation is being used legally and, where there is uncertainty about the status or ownership of particular information, recommendations for appropriate risk-mitigating policies.

More generally, the use of information audits should not be viewed as a chore, but rather as part of a continuous improvement/enhancement approach in all that the organisation does, as well as maximising the value of its information assets.

Information and records are received and created by staff members and others to facilitate and support the organisation's business processes; they are the inputs and outputs of the organisation's activities. Ensuring that the information assets are managed correctly should lead to improvements in the efficiency of the organisation's business processes. So, an information audit not only ensures legislative compliance, but also helps the organisation to:

- develop, where appropriate, an information asset register (IAR) and/or develop/update records retention schedules (RRS), both of which are compliance assurance tools

◆ inform the development of policies and procedures to help improve the management of information and records
◆ generally raise awareness of the importance of good information and records management practices, and the requirements and individuals' responsibilities in this regard.

There are not just benefits for the organisation as a whole; others will benefit:

◆ for staff, knowledge that the right information is available to the right people at the right time, and an assurance that all the information they encounter is legitimately obtained, reliable, secure and authentic, and can be easily found and retrieved for use and reuse
◆ for other stakeholders, confidence that the organisation takes its responsibilities towards information governance and records management very seriously and that their data is safe and secure with the organisation.

The audit process involves five stages, which are described below. For any given piece of information (or coherent group of information), one should go through the steps in order. One should also be prepared to repeat the process as often as is appropriate for the particular information involved – perhaps on an annual basis. It is important to document what was done and what the results were for each stage for each content group, so that updating or reviewing the content becomes straightforward.

It could also be that significant changes in the law relating to some of the information might occur. If this is the case, the review should take place in anticipation of the change of law, once the shape of the revised law becomes clear. A watching brief should then be maintained, including checking the changes to the law as they occur, and keeping track of informed commentaries regarding the implications of the revised law. If a significant legal case results in a judgment that has implications for the organisation's information policy, then of course a rapid review of current policies should take place and, if necessary, the policies should be amended and/or the information should be deleted, amended or added to as necessary.

Stage One: identifying the rights

Audit the various types of right that might subsist in the content the organisation uses or wishes to use. These can include: copyright; database right; performers' rights and unregistered and registered trade marks. Of course, bear in mind which information might be subject to FoI and data protection laws as well. There are numerous texts, which provide guidance on the various intellectual property rights and on FoI and data protection matters. We like Padfield (2019) and Cornish (2019) as user-friendly practical approaches to the law of copyright, and Michaels and Norris (2014) on trade marks. Jay's work on data protection law and practice and the GDPR (2017), together with other works noted in Chapter 2 and Carey (2018) are recommended. Gibbons (2019) *The Freedom of Information Officer's Handbook* is also recommended.

If not previously carried out, the process involves questionnaires to all relevant personnel in the organisation. This will probably be followed by a collation and assessment exercise, with subsequent identification of any areas that look high risk or where not enough is known about the information and further questions are required. There should, of course, be a particular emphasis on identifying that information that is consumed or created, which involves personal data, or is commercially valuable. The questionnaire should also identify the business activity and retention period for each type of information, as well as security, accessibility, procedures, policies (such as records retention schedules), training, awareness and responsibilities.

Stage Two: calculate the duration of the rights

When considering data protection, legal obligations continue for as long as any identifiable individual who forms part of the record is still alive, so it is best to assume that data protection applies to any personal data that is less than 100 years old. There are of course many exemptions that can be applied should a complaint regarding data protection, or an SAR be made, but the default position that should be adopted is that everything held by the organisation that is less than 100 years old containing personal information is potentially subject to data protection laws. It is worth noting that under the GDPR, most organisations are required to carry out, and maintain records of, personal information that is processed. So, in the case of data protection, there really is no choice but to carry out a fully documented information audit at regular intervals. Furthermore, all staff need to be reminded of the relatively new requirement that breaches of the Data Protection Act 2018 must be reported to the ICO.

There is no time limit to the applicability of FoI law, so if your organisation is one that is subject to the law, you should assume that all information held by the organisation is potentially subject to FoI requests. As has been noted in Chapter 3, there are many exemptions that can be applied, but the default position should be that FoI law potentially applies to everything held by your organisation.

Turning to trade marks, both registered and unregistered, their lifetime is potentially indefinite so long as renewal fees (in the case of registered trade marks) are paid. If the mark is owned by your organisation, the appropriate legal unit within it should be able to confirm whether the mark is still in force or not, and what classes of goods and services it covers. If one is dealing with third-party marks, the UK IPO can confirm if a particular registered mark is still in force or has expired, but there is no single source of information on unregistered marks owned by third parties, so a risk-averse organisation will no doubt wish to assume they are still in force and should not be using them without permission.

The lifetime of copyright works varies according to the particular type of work involved. Thus, the lifetime of literary works, artistic works, music, sound recordings, films, dramatic works and broadcasts vary between each genre; database rights, moral rights and performers' rights also have special rules for their lifetimes. Bear in mind that any particular item or collection may well have different types of works embedded within them, possibly created by different individuals or organisations, so untangling their lifetimes can be difficult. The lifetime of unpublished works, or photographs, and of orphan works are particularly difficult to calculate, and so a risk-managed approach may well be required. More details about lifetimes can be found in Chapter 1, or in standard texts.

Stage Three: identify who owns the rights

Of course, employees carrying out their employee duties will have created much of the information owned by an organisation. Copyright in virtually all such materials automatically belongs to the organisation.[4] Inevitably,

---

4. There may be an exception to this rule if employees have created a performance, such as a lecture, in the course of their duties. In these cases, the performer's right typically belongs to the employee.

though, there will be other types of content, such as that provided by freelancers, by students (perhaps on placement), volunteers, employees but not as part of their employee duties, commercial content suppliers, clients of the organisation, others who have some kind of relationship with the organisation, representatives of rights holders, etc. In some cases, the owner may be unknown.

Stage Four: establish what rights and permissions and exceptions or exemptions your organisation may benefit from

It is crucial that before working out whether permission is necessary and as a precursor of a potential rights clearance strategy, you identify what agreements you already have in place (licences, consents, permissions and/or assignments) and/or whether you can benefit from specific exceptions and exemptions, to enable you to use the work in the ways that you would like. This information may be held on content and/or collection management systems, digital asset management systems, spreadsheets, in e-mails, filing cabinets and sometimes in archived files and analogue and digital files. The copyright officer and/or DPO will also be an important source of information about any exceptions and/or exemptions to legal compliance obligations that might apply.

Stage Five: develop next steps, including rights and/or permissions clearance requirements and any risk management approaches, including risk mitigation strategies

These will vary from organisation to organisation, and will reflect both the potential problem issues that have been identified and time, costs and resources available, as well as the organisation's appetite for risk. It will be clear from this account that undertaking an audit of information held by the organisation and then working out what can and cannot be done with such items, and the levels of risk involved, will involve significant time and effort. The level of detail that your organisation decides to invest in the effort depends very much on the results of a preliminary analysis of what is held, what is being done with the materials and how likely such use or planned use is to be problematic, as well as identifying any outstanding information needs of the organisation. This should be carried out by someone familiar with the holdings and needs, and with information law – that is to say, very often a LIK worker.

Of course, one should always remember that any given piece of information may comprise several types of rights, and may well be subject to data protection legislation as well. All these factors need to be identified and highlighted if necessary.

All the more care and detailed evaluation is needed if your organisation currently exploits, or plans to exploit, some of its, or a third party's, information assets commercially. Consideration also needs to be given regarding how risk-averse the organisation is – a factor that is tied to the risk of reputational as well as financial damage. If your organisation owns trade marks, whether registered or unregistered, then specific strategies and policies should be developed for the protection and exploitation of said assets. It is likely that these matters will be part of the remit of the legal or the marketing department of the organisation, but it is best to double-check that this is, in fact, the case. If not, then the LIK management unit may well be the place to carry out such audits.

One result from this stage may be the development of recommendations to improve the quality of data about the information held or needed. If this is the case, this improvement process should be included in the organisation's forward/action planning. See Appendix 1 for an example of how to carry out an information asset audit.

Case study 4.2: Information asset audit for a digitisation project

An information service wishes to digitise and publish online its back catalogues of feminist magazines using public funding. Prior to establishing a rights clearance strategy, as well as an evaluation of the use of any of the exceptions to copyright, it carries out an information asset audit to ascertain what permissions are required and upon the basis of this, cost out the necessary time, money and staff resources required to carry out the clearance work as a substantive part of the project management and resource management components of the project.

Forward planning

If the organisation does not already have a co-ordinated information governance strategy, this should be a priority, as information governance frameworks and policies should be based on the strategic priorities as well as legal compliance. The information governance strategy should set out strategic and operational responsibilities. The results of a systematic audit will inform the process by identifying what policies and procedures are already in place, how effective they are given the organisation's strategic priorities and what needs to be done to ensure alignment with these priorities and legal compliance, including the creation of guidance and training for staff.

When governance structures are formalised and in place, a detailed plan of what actions must be carried out, by whom, for what purpose, and when and how progress will be monitored, can be drawn up within the organisation. This plan will require input and buy-in across the organisation. If a comprehensive and up-to-date framework of policies is not already in place, this will be a priority. Information law policies are discussed in the next chapter. Procedures will also need to be put in place, reviewed, or modified as appropriate to ensure compliance with organisational policies. Such procedures are discussed in Chapters 6, 7 and 8.

Top tips

1   Integrating an effective 'rights and privacy by design' culture requires suitable information governance frameworks.
2   There may well be copyright exceptions and FoI/data protection exemptions, which apply to the use of, and/or access to, information.
3   At the very least, a nominated data protection and copyright organisational lead is essential to ensure oversight of legal compliance issues and to ensure that issues are reported back to senior management as appropriate.
4   Information law compliance requires a top-down and bottom-up organisational commitment supported by an appropriate information governance framework.
5   Audits are a vital component in evaluating the issues and helping to establish the next steps in information and data management and use.

5

Policies

Introduction

In this chapter, we will cover why it is important to develop policies relating to information law, what a typical policy might contain, what the key areas that should be covered by such policies are, such as risk management, dealing with complaints, consent management, ownership of rights and use of third-party content.

It is not difficult to make the case for the need for formal policies, whatever the size of the organisation or of its LIK management function. LIK workers are likely to be managing copyright and permissions associated with access to print and electronic resources on a daily basis, and are likely to be involved in issues relating to FoI requests and/or data protection issues on a regular or irregular basis. This means that proficiency and awareness of these topics is increasingly a requirement of their skills set. A lack of a basic understanding of copyright and database rights, or of FoI or data protection law, can restrict access to information and resources, could be detrimental to an organisation's ability to maximise the impact and/or exploitation of IPR that it owns, as well as putting the organisation at risk because of its failure to comply with its contractual or legal obligations. Other risks relate, for example, to users or staff copying more than they should, using materials in ways they should not or viewing, sharing or downloading inappropriate/illegal material, or the organisation giving incorrect advice or failing to respond correctly to an SAR or a FoI request.

The key risks for an organisation not getting its policies right, or having appropriate policies but staff ignoring them, are:

- breaking the law
- more stress and uncertainty than necessary
- potential financial penalties
- potential damage to reputation
- increased pressures on resources
- discontented users who no longer make use of the services, cause problems, or bad-mouth the organisation to third parties
- job losses/disciplinary procedures
- an over-cautious approach, which leads to frustration for others, or failing to grasp opportunities that present themselves.

It is clear that the business case for putting relevant policies in place is extremely strong. Clear, well-understood policies will result in:

- cost savings by providing the framework for streamlined and rapid processes responding to issues that arise
- reduced risk of copyright infringement, or breaking the legal requirements imposed by FoI and/or data protection legislation
- reduced risk of costs or penalties incurred because of mistakes made through ignorance of what was required
- reduced risk of reputational damage caused by negative publicity associated with events that occurred where the organisation was at fault
- creation of transparent and clearly worded instructions to staff
- demonstrating to funders, partners, suppliers, clients/patrons and other third parties that the organisation is professionally run and takes its legal obligations seriously.

The general approach adopted should include the following factors:

- acceptance that rights management = risk management
- an understanding of the nature and extent of risks, and taking steps that are both proportionate and informed
- organisational risk mitigation activities are key
- most people (staff and patrons) want to do the right thing
- policies can make it easier for them to do so, but not police in an intrusive manner

◆ but just in case of problems, there is a need for provisions to reduce or mitigate potentially bad effects on the organisation in place.

There is no standard way of producing an appropriate policy for an organisation and such policies can appear in a variety of shapes and sizes. However, policies should take a number of factors into account:

◆ The policy should result from involvement and engagement with staff within the organisation at all levels, and not just be imposed top down. In particular, it should reflect and take advantage of the culture of the organisation, rather than be developed without staff buy-in.
◆ It should consider all the issues that are important to the organisation.
◆ It should be embedded within the organisation's framework of policies to ensure consistency with them.
◆ It should reflect the direction that the organisation is taking or plans to take in terms of its priorities and engagement with third parties.
◆ It should reflect the organisation's appetite for risk.
◆ It should include incentives, and not just penalties, to encourage compliance.
◆ Where it is felt that cultural change is necessary, the development of novel provisions to encourage such a change.
◆ It should include the appropriate balance between compliance, ethics and pragmatism.

Developing an appropriate policy with staff buy-in can only be achieved through a combined top-down, bottom-up approach, i.e. one that is supported at an operational level for staff awareness and training as appropriate, as well as staff feeling they have been involved in the development of the policy, combined with an understanding of the corporate culture and of the organisation's direction of travel. Without taking these factors into account, the policy will become a document that is at best not understood and at worst deliberately ignored.

What should the policy contain?

The purpose of an information law policy is to identify clear roles and responsibilities for staff, the senior management team/board, patrons, students, contractors, volunteers (if any) plus any other third parties who might interact with the organisation. It should identify key rights concerns and issues facing them and the organisation. It should ensure that all the organisation's legal responsibilities are articulated but in a way that balances practical risk assessment with the needs and plans of the organisation. It will provide an articulation of principles relating to information rights and responsibilities. Most importantly, it will provide a framework for an approach to rights-related issues so that mistakes are not made and there is an identifiable consistency and chain of responsibility that can be demonstrated should problems arise. This could be linked to a logbook of incidents and requests, with a report of how they were handled and what consequences resulted.

We recommend that separate policies be developed: one for copyright and any other relevant intellectual property rights, one for data protection, and one for FoI (if applicable to the organisation). Various topics could be covered in the policies, depending on the nature of the organisation and the information it holds, or would wish to access.

For copyright and database right (see Appendix 2 for a sample IP policy)

◆   ownership of IPR
◆   use made of materials whose IPR is owned by third party rights
◆   permissions for third parties to use institutional IP
◆   management of IPR, including protection of IP owned by the organisation
◆   access to content held by the organisation
◆   crediting third parties
◆   approach taken when an organisation's IPR has been infringed
◆   dealing with orphan works
◆   'notice and take-down' policy and procedures
◆   possibly performers' rights, Public Lending Right and other related rights which may be applicable
◆   dealing with moral rights
◆   who is empowered to make decisions on these matters
◆   dealing with complaints/allegations of infringement
◆   links to sources of information, such as the UK IPO's website.

These should further be supported by:

◆ notices such as signage for self-service copying on walls and on desks and in spaces in between everywhere copying/access takes place
◆ information on websites
◆ terms and conditions for access to digital content fully explained
◆ acceptable use policies (AUPs) for internet sites (children/adults)
◆ risk registers, action plans and risk books.

For data protection (see Appendix 3 for a sample data protection policy)

◆ contact details for the DPO (assuming there is one), or of any other person responsible for data protection matters
◆ whereabouts of data protection impact assessments (see Chapter 8)/information audit results
◆ whereabouts of registers of activities which have data protection implications
◆ methods of prioritising significance of data protection-related activities
◆ development of, and updating, all public statements relevant to data protection
◆ recognising what is, or is not, a data protection-related request, complaint or potentially problematic activity
◆ links to relevant sources of information, such as the UK ICO's website
◆ links to all internal documents relating to procedures, including any template forms for use by staff and/or third parties
◆ links to any codes of practice developed internally
◆ links to any relevant training materials/details of compliance systems.

These should further be supported by:

◆ suitable signage on walls and elsewhere
◆ information on websites
◆ AUPs

◆ risk registers
◆ action plans and risk book.

For freedom of information

◆ information held by the organisation/where information asset registers are maintained
◆ details of the contents of any public-facing websites
◆ recognising what is, and is not, an FoI request, who deals with such requests within the organisation, and what types of information held by the organisation are exempt from disclosure, e.g., those that conflict with data protection requirements
◆ who is empowered to make decisions on these matters
◆ dealing with complaints
◆ links to sources of information, such as the ICO's website
◆ reminders of time limits to respond to requests.

For all three, there needs to be a recognition that the strands can, and do, often overlap and are sometimes in conflict with one another, and where to seek advice on how one should resolve such conflicts.

How does one ensure the policies work?

Any information law-related policy is only as good as the extent to which it is recognised and adopted by all staff within the organisation. This can be achieved by a combination of methods that work best in an individual organisation's culture and size. Some of the approaches work well within an organisation that is in a single location; others are more appropriate for organisations with a widely scattered workforce, including, of course, staff who work from home. This workforce can include full-time employees, part-time employees and/or freelancers and contractors. Even the latter group – indeed, especially the latter group – needs to be made aware of the relevant policies. Readers are encouraged to consider the culture and circumstances of their own organisation before deciding which approach to take. Chapter 10 provides details about awareness and training matters.

The most important requirement is to have the active support of the most senior level of management within the organisation. Beyond that, consider one or more of the following: regular staff training and awareness raising; having the key contacts as very public, well-known individuals who are respected at all levels; and establish a working party for each, or all, of the issues involving staff at all levels of seniority. Furthermore, the general tenor of any policy documents must be clear, friendly and supportive, and should not be overly threatening. However, somewhere it does need to be made clear that the organisation's finances and reputation are potentially at risk if a serious breach occurs, and that therefore reckless or illegal behaviours by a member of staff in regard to these matters could be considered as a possible disciplinary offence. Incidentally, depending on the size and nature of the organisation, senior management should consider having one individual fulfilling the three roles of DPO, FoI contact and copyright contact. Chapter 4 discusses the importance of information governance and various frameworks, which can be established in an organisation to support information law compliance and the associated policies.

At a more detailed level, the policies should give guidance on the steps that should be taken to research and acquire rights, or to respond to a request; the steps needed to evaluate potential contracts that the organisation might enter into, including of course, in the case of acquiring access to digital resources, the nature of the licence, the fees payable, and the general acceptability of any terms and conditions imposed. More on this particular topic can be found in Chapter 7.

As has been repeatedly stressed in this book, one of the major problems with information law is the ambiguous nature of terms used in legislation that are open to interpretation, and are sometimes the subject of court cases. These include terms such as 'substantial' (or 'insubstantial'), 'fair' (especially as in 'fair dealing'), 'published', 'dedicated terminals', 'justifiable', 'adequate', 'commercial' (and of course 'non-commercial') and 'reasonable'. Any written policy can give informal guidance on how the law should be interpreted, but this will never be formal legal advice. In cases of doubt, the puzzled employee should seek the advice of whoever is designated as the expert on the law within the organisation, rather than attempt to decide the answer for themselves.

Throughout the development of policies, the organisation should take into account the balance between the risks of some thing going wrong, the costs of implementing particular policies, and the benefits to the organisation of implementing said policies. These factors are difficult to quantify, but some effort should be made, taking into account, as always, the appetite for risk that the organisation has and its willingness to spend money on policies that require significant investment of staff time, in new systems, etc. Negative aspects of a policy also need to be considered: for example, whether particular policies will slow down the day-to-day workings of the organisation and its reputation for friendliness, and efficiency. A heavily bureaucratic, but very safe, approach would not necessarily be appropriate for all organisations in all circumstances, for example.

Information policy examples

The following examples illustrate how information law policies can be used to manage specific IPR and licensing, data protection and FoI pressure points.

♦ **Example 1:** A research library stating that it is committed to complying with the terms of various blanket and electronic licences for accessing print and electronic resources and pointing to various procedures and tools created to help achieve this.
♦ **Example 2:** A university that states that undergraduate students retain the copyright in any work they produce, and where appropriate, grant the university a non-commercial licence to reuse their work. However, the term 'non-commercial' may be open to conflicting interpretations.
♦ **Example 3:** A cultural heritage organisation that develops a policy on orphan works and risk management to support its digitisation programme.
♦ **Example 4:** A health library that develops a policy statement on open access.
♦ **Example 5:** A funding body states that its funding recipients can retain any copyright in outputs arising from the funding, as long as the recipients make such outputs available under open access principles. This raises questions regarding whether the policy applies to early drafts, or final published outputs.
♦ **Example 6:** A college that develops a benefit-sharing model for teaching materials created by staff and exploited by the college. The policy makes clear that the member of staff cannot further exploit the materials in any private teaching they undertake, or should they move to another job.

◆ **Example 7:** A law firm's library that informs Partners that they must take responsibility for ensuring that their copying activities are lawful. (The reputational damage for a law firm that is found to have infringed copyright would be very great).

◆ **Example 8:** A public library that requires that users of its Wi-Fi service sign up to acceptable use policies at the beginning of each session.

◆ **Example 9:** A charity develops an infringement policy with reference to a notice and take-down policy and procedures to mitigate its risks when publishing third party generated digital resources.

◆ **Example 10:** An archive that produces a photography and scanning policy for visiting researchers.

◆ **Example 11:** A group of pubic libraries under the control of two adjacent local authorities decides to use a single DPO. The DPO's tasks include visiting each library in turn at regular intervals to assess compliance with the GDPR.

◆ **Example 12:** The library/information service for a large pharmaceutical company carries out an assessment and concludes none of the data its holds is subject to FoI.

◆ **Example 13:** The library of a large law firm produces guidance on how to handle SARs and in particular, how to assess whether it needs to respond to them, and how to handle those where the decision is not to provide the information requested.

◆ **Example 14:** A school library develops a template for individuals, including pupils, parents or carers, to use when exercising their rights to carry out a SAR.

◆ **Example 15:** A university develops guidance for dealing with student and former student requests to see comments made about them (including references written and comments on dissertations and exam answers) by staff whilst they were at the university.

This list of examples just gives a flavour of the many types of policy documents that might be produced by an organisation.

Checklist for an information law policy

There is no single way of producing an information law policy; as we have stressed, they come in all shapes and sizes, depending on the circumstances, size and culture of the organisation. For this reason, it would be inappropriate for a book such as this to suggest definitive recommended policy wording, rather than just the general template policies provided in the appendices. Nonetheless, we suggest that certain basic ground rules are followed. Ideally any information law policy should:

◆ reflect the current culture, and the ongoing cultural change within the organisation, rather than using a policy document as a tool to change the culture

◆ reflect comments made during previous engagement with staff, rather than being developed in isolation and without staff buy-in

◆ be holistic – the policy document needs to consider all the issues that are important across the organisation regarding the use of its assets, as well as those belonging to third parties

◆ reflect the priorities and sensitivities of the organisation, and in particular pay particular attention to areas of big concern, such as processing of sensitive personal data, or the retention of control over particularly valuable assets, including key copyrights or registered trade marks

◆ in the case of IPR, be broken down into headings such as identifying rights holders of third-party materials, acquiring rights to use or reproduce when needed, protecting the rights that we own, carrying out a rights audit, dealing with complaints, identifying issues in contracts about to be signed, taking advantage of exceptions to copyright and CC licences, and dealing with orphan works

◆ in the case of data protection, be broken down into headings such as what processes involve personal data, what to do when sensitive personal data is involved, identifying issues in contracts about to be signed, detailed evaluation of where personal information might be transferred to, justifications for processing personal data, when you should check with the DPO on what you are doing, how to recognise and deal with a SAR, data protection issues to look out for in any contracts entered into, how to recognise a data protection complaint, security issues to be considered, and rules about use of memory sticks or working with personal data away from the organisation's premises

◆ be embedded within the organisation's broad policy framework to ensure consistency with existing governance frameworks and policies; particular attention should be given to areas where different aspects of information law might conflict with each other, e.g., FoI versus data protection

- ◆ reflect the approach that an organisation is taking in terms of its appetite for risk, and its balancing of access priorities and partnership engagements
- ◆ form part of a broader compliance framework, as outlined in Chapter 4
- ◆ include incentives and not just penalties to support willing compliance
- ◆ take account of insurance policies that the organisation has taken out, and identify potential gaps in insurance cover
- ◆ identify requirements for awareness and training.

6 Procedures: copyright and related rights

Introduction

Information policies set out an organisation's objectives with regard to management of information, including IPR management. Organisations must also develop procedures to achieve these objectives. Procedures should be designed not only to implement policies, but also to do so effectively and as efficiently as possible. Information policies are organisation-wide, but procedures may have to be tailored to reflect the respective roles and responsibilities of different functions within the organisation. It should be assumed that procedures are likely to adapt to their environment and thus change more frequently than policies. Staff will implement procedures, but other stakeholders, such as contractors, agents, customers, users or visitors, will also have a part to play.

A core purpose of information policy is to ensure legal compliance and accountability, and procedures should reflect this. Other considerations include the protection and/or exploitation of information assets, a commitment to good service, reputation and fairness and transparency. This means that procedures will have to be nuanced to suit each purpose. For example, an educational institution's IPR management procedures may differ depending on whether creators are staff, doctoral researchers, taught students, visiting academics or independent contractors. Access to personal data will depend on job role and purpose. Provision of information by public bodies will depend on the nature of this information and the public interest.

Procedures should be developed to ensure that appropriate decisions and actions are taken, that the decision-making process is timely and transparent and that decisions and agreements are appropriately documented. Procedures should ensure clarity in responsibilities and the order in which activities and decisions are taken. In this chapter, we set out the various procedures that should be put in place by organisations to implement IPR policy.

Intellectual property rights

An IPR policy will address ownership of IPR and related rights and use of third-party IPR. It will also specify the underlying values and objectives for how IPR is managed within the organisation. Both of these aspects of policy will be reflected in procedures. IPR management will overlap with other areas of policy and related procedures, including induction and training, disciplinary procedures and acceptable-use policies for technology and systems. Ownership of IPR should be dealt with in written agreements, such as employment contracts, rights transfer and licence agreements and other contractual arrangements. The organisation's attitude towards ownership and use of IP should be reflected in the provisions of standard agreements. There may be some flexibility in procedures. For example, research institutions may wish to exploit industrial property, including patents, commercially, while taking (or being forced by funders to take) an open approach to dissemination and use of research outputs or educational resources. Agreements should also be used to grant permissions to third parties to use the organisation's IPR. There may be both legal and ethical dimensions here. For example, different approaches to exploitation of IPR may be taken depending on whether the requested use is commercial or not. This may manifest itself in whether and what fees are charged for use.

Procedures will also be implemented to ensure compliance with the terms of agreements between organisations and their suppliers, staff and external service users or clients. Awareness is discussed in Chapter 10 of this book. Organisations should take steps to ensure all concerned are aware of their rights and responsibilities. This can be done, for example, through staff handbooks, acceptable use policies, information for visitors, notices close to copying facilities and on intranets or virtual learning environments, and through training.

Library, information and knowledge services and intellectual property rights

LIK workers are likely to be most concerned with copyright and these rights are therefore the focus of this chapter. Related rights, particularly database, moral and performance rights should also be considered in procedures. LIK services will be directly involved in aspects of rights management, including managing institutional repositories, subscriptions to information services, licence negotiation, providing access to resources and supporting staff and user compliance with the law and legal agreements that have been entered into. LIK service units should maintain documentation of all licence agreements and declarations in writing associated with the supply of content, as well as agreements with collective rights management agencies and service suppliers. Such a collection of agreements and associated correspondence could be indexed, for example, by name of the service, relevant contact details, the date the agreement was signed and when it is due to expire. Then if a query arises relating to contractual terms or renewal negotiations, these can be quickly checked. Records of issues raised during the previous negotiations and how they were resolved (assuming they were) could also be documented.

Compliance can be enforced through technological protection and security measures to prevent infringing behaviour. For other activities, such as photocopying, and downloading from the internet, direct monitoring of behaviour presents an ethical dilemma. This makes procedures for raising and maintaining awareness of crucial importance. Organisations should also develop procedures for detecting and dealing with infringements of their own IPR. The media industries are particularly committed to this approach for obvious reasons and work with online platforms to detect and require the take-down of infringing material. LIK services may not be heavily involved in this activity, as they are more concerned with ensuring lawful use of the information services they provide. However, they should work with their users to ensure any material deposited in any institutional stores or repositories by users is lawful.

Case study 6.1: The consequences of not having rights management procedures

Commercial Image Supplier approaches University Y stating that several images up on the university's website infringe copyright, and appropriate fees should be paid. University Y originally sourced the images from the internet and had not sought permission for images to be used in the first place. University Y does not respond. Very shortly after this, Commercial Image Supplier demands immediate take-down. University Y does not respond. Commercial Image Supplier swiftly sends University Y an invoice for several times the initial amount and threats of naming and shaming. University Y liaises with in-house legal team, who had not been contacted until this point, and the payment is settled.

Orphan works

LIK services may wish to increase access to materials in their collections through digitisation. For material still in copyright, this will involve both carrying out restricted acts in copyright law, and potential infringement of related rights. These services must seek permission from rights holders to carry out any activities on materials that are still in copyright that are not covered by current licences or copyright exceptions. A specialist unit may carry out copyright clearance, or the service may have to do this. If there is a dedicated copyright officer, they may well take on this role or at least devise the procedures and oversee the process of copyright clearance. It may also be possible to use external copyright clearance and digitisation services. Whatever approach is taken, it will require full and accurate details of the works to be digitised, the uses that are envisaged, and the time the rights are required for. Contact details of rights holders or their representatives need to be found and records kept of all correspondence between the parties. Agreements must be in writing and kept safe and easily accessible.

In the case of orphan works, by definition, rights holders are untraceable or unknown. UK copyright law makes some provisions for calculating the copyright term for anonymous or pseudonymous works. This is quite straightforward if the year of creation or publication is known. Anonymous or pseudonymous literary, dramatic, artistic or musical works that are available to the public are protected for 70 years from when they were first made available. Copyright in unpublished works created on or after 1969 expires

70 years after the creation date (Copyright, Designs and Patents Act 1988, s. 12(3)). Copyright in unpublished works, whether anonymous, pseudonymous or known authors, created before 1969 will not expire until 31 December 2039 (Copyright, Designs and Patents Act 1988, schedule 1, s. 12).

Difficulties arise where creation or publication dates are not known. Research will be then be required to attempt to identify anonymous or pseudonymous authors, determine whether they are still alive or when they died, determine if they are in fact the rights holders and who to contact to ask for permissions. Some categories of copyright work are more likely to raise complications. For example, photographic material is more likely to be orphaned because photographers are not always acknowledged or recorded. There may be multiple rights holders in audiovisual material, who all have to be identified. Unpublished letters, manuscripts and diaries can pose particularly problematic issues because of the overly lengthy duration of copyright in certain items (until the end of the year 2039) regardless of their age, and therefore present a greater likelihood of being orphan works.

LIK services may decide to only digitise material that is clearly out of copyright to avoid the resource-intensive process of finding rights holders and clearing rights, but this presents important ethical issues about the self-censoring of history and the creation of black holes of cultural heritage information. Regardless, procedures for dealing with orphan works should be informed by the relevant legal provisions that were mentioned in Chapter 1. The first is the orphan works exception in copyright law (Copyright and Rights in Performances (Certain Permitted Uses of Orphan Works) Regulations 2014). This allows cultural and heritage organisations, which include some publicly accessible libraries and archives, to digitise and make orphan works available for non-commercial purposes only. However, the exception does not include standalone artistic works. What is more, readers should be aware that the UK IPO (2018a) has warned that this provision will not be retained if the UK exits the EU without a deal because it was introduced through the EU's Orphan Works Directive (2012/28/EU).

An alternative is to ask for a licence through the UK IPO's orphan works licensing scheme.[1] Orphan works licences can be granted for commercial purposes, but may be of limited use to library and information services,

---

1. www.gov.uk/guidance/copyright-orphan-works

particularly for mass-digitisation projects. The licences are limited to the UK and last seven years (although they can be renewed). The IPO recommends a set of procedures to follow before applying for such a licence. These include investigating the copyright status of works and whether any exceptions apply to the proposed use. The next stage is to carry out a 'diligent search' to identify the rights holders. The Intellectual Property Office (2015a) provides guidance on how to apply for such a licence and what information should be included in the application. There are also guides to what constitutes a diligent search for different categories of copyright work (Intellectual Property Office, 2018b). Twenty-seven licences were granted for 247 works in the first year of the scheme. Twenty of the licences were for non-commercial use. Although this is a small number of applications, the majority of applicants were satisfied with the application process (Intellectual Property Office, 2015b). No further annual reports have been published on the IPO website, so it is not clear whether the scheme is well-used. Research on the issue suggests that it is not useful for cultural heritage institutions (Callaghan 2017; Stobo et al. 2018, 22; Martinez and Terras, 2019).

Rights management means risk management

It cannot be stressed too much, and hence its repetition in this book, that handling copyright problems is as much to do with management of risk as it is to do with the law. Risk management is crucial in deciding whether to use something that is in (or is likely to be in) copyright and for which you do not have permissions, whether it is an orphan work and/or within the context of using the exceptions to copyright. Sometimes risk management is fundamental in deciding whether the item is even in copyright or not, because of what it is. The vast and eclectic range of items held across the cultural heritage sector, including libraries and archives, also presents challenges. For example, amongst other categories of works, copyright protects 'artistic works'. Hence, can Tracy Emin's artwork 'My Bed' 1998, comprised of her unmade bed, or indeed Marcel Duchamp's 'Fountain' 1917, comprised of a urinal, be classed as sculptures and subsequently shoe-horned into copyright protection?

It is important to have a strategy towards risk. There are three parts to the risk management strategy: calculation of the risks, the cost/benefit calculation, and your (or your employer's) appetite for risk. Of course, knowledge of the law is needed, but, as we have noted, there are too many vague words (such as 'substantial', 'the public' 'normal exploitation', 'commercial', 'reasonable', etc.) employed in the legislation and by courts for certainty regarding a particular use. Copyright law is not always black and white and if, for example, significant efforts have been made to trace the copyright owner, and this can be backed up with evidence, then it is up to the organisation planning to exploit a copyright work to calculate the risk and decide if this is mitigated by the research it has undertaken. It is important to make sure that the cost of obtaining copyright or licensed use does not exceed the benefit of using the item. As noted previously, when there are several layers of rights to assess, or large amounts of research needed to establish, for example, who the owner of the copyright is, there are costs in terms of time as well as monetary value.

For an organisation, being risk-aware requires a corporate decision on its approach to risk decided by the senior management team and embedded within the governance framework (discussed in Chapter 4), as well as supported by appropriate policy statements (Chapter 5). However, this needs to be supported by an organisation-wide commitment in place, because ultimately, risk management is only as good as the provisions in place to mitigate and ideally neutralise any risk. These include:

1   A widely understood notice and take-down procedure. This is of course not so easy in the case of printed publications. It is crucial to record all the processes carried out before reproducing any potentially problematic item. All relevant types of rights, not just copyright, need to be considered (see further below).
2   Appropriate indemnity insurance to cover any infringement claims. It is worth checking to see whether such insurance exists, for example, in the terms of any existing insurance policies maintained by the organisation, before making any enquiries about obtaining a policy tied to information law indemnity.
3   Being risk-averse within the context of reasonable searches, which means more effort has to be put into trying to track and document rights holders. For example, it involves checking things online, contacting organisations that might be able to help, etc.
4   As part of the planning process for any project, decisions will be needed as to how the technology and content is to be made available – whether freely available to all, or only from behind technological

protection measures (TPMs)/password-protected sites; i.e. only for use by the community you serve. While the route chosen will not change liability should copyright be infringed (i.e. infringing content behind a password-protected site will still infringe) the circulation of the content is more limited where circulation/distribution of content is restricted by technical controls. Where circulation is limited, this could inform decisions, for example, as to whether an orphan work should be used.

Ultimately, it is important that you are proportionate about possible risks, whilst at the same time prepare suitable mitigating strategies in the eventuality that a rights holder does complain. For some organisations, reputational risk is more important than financial risk. An organisation's approach to risk can be articulated in a copyright risk management plan.[2]

Our general advice when deciding to copy or carry out some other restricted act with an in-copyright work is to do the following:

- Check if the organisation already has a licence that would cover the proposed action. If it does, go ahead.
- If not, check if an exception to copyright applies. If it does, go ahead.
- If not, adopt a risk management approach. If the risk is low, consider going ahead and using the work.
- If the risk is high, try to get permission from the copyright owner to use the materials.
- If the risk is high and the rights owner does not reply, denies permission or demands an unreasonable sum for permission, don't use the materials. There may be an alternative work that could be used instead.

Note that, as we have stressed elsewhere, risk management includes not just the financial risk (of being sued, for example), but also the reputational risk of being perceived as having a cavalier attitude to copyright. The risk is also dependent on whether the use made of the item is commercial or non-commercial; whether distribution is online or by print; the size of the potential audience; and whether the original work was an orphan work or

---

2. Copyrightlaws.com provides some useful advice on developing a copyright risk management plan: www.copyrightlaws.com/developing-copyright-risk-management-plan.

not. Table 6.1 summarises the situation regarding risk based on these factors. Different individuals and organisations will have different appetites for risk.

Table 6.1 Risk factors in copyright infringement		
	Higher risk	**Lower risk**
Commercial exploitation	x	
Non-commercial exploitation		x
Online distribution	x	
Print distribution		x
Large audience	x	
Small audience		x
Orphan original		x
Non-orphan original	x	

There are several ways that have been developed over the years to try and 'quantify' these risks and as a result develop informed and pragmatic ways to handle third-party copyright materials, including orphan works. The formula in Figure 6.1 has been created to assess the level of risk involved.

$R =$ $A \times B \times C \times D$
    Where **R** is the financial risk
$A =$ chance of infringement
$B =$ chance of awareness of any infringement by a copyright owner
$C =$ chance of action by an aggrieved copyright owner
$D =$ is the financial cost, e.g. damages awarded, expenditure on legal advice, costs awarded, increased insurance premiums

Figure 6.1 *Formula for quantifying risk factors in copyright infringement*

In the formula, **A** is 1 (i.e. 100%) when there can be little doubt that using someone else's copyright material for a commercial purpose can be seen as an infringement. It is less than 1 if there is uncertainty as to whether what is being done is infringement or not, e.g., when an exception to copyright might apply.

B will vary depending on the use the material is put to. Of course, the more the allegedly infringing material is distributed, the more likely it is that this will come to the notice of the copyright owner. **B** can range between, say, 0.001 (very low chance) to 1 (certain to occur).

C is also likely to vary depending on any commercial aspect the material is used for and who the rights holder is. Some rights holders are far more aggressive about suing for infringement than others, and for such aggressive owners, the figure should be put at 1.

D is potentially a high number. There is a strong argument that no case should ever go to court, but that if sued, an offer to make amends should be made and a contingency fund set aside for these circumstances. We are aware of cases such as Bentley Clothing versus Bentley Motors (2019)[3] relating to trade mark infringement rather than copyright, where the aggrieved party invited the alleged infringer to pay a small sum, the alleged infringer refused such a deal, the matter went to court, and the infringer is now required to pay hundreds of thousands of pounds in damages.

N.B. No calculation can be realistically made for loss of reputation. In some circumstances, the reputational damage can be considerably higher than the notional financial costs. Reputational damage might be reflected in share price, loss of sales, loss of partners or of co-operation with rights holders, departure of key staff, increased insurance premiums payable or a lower credit rating for the organisation.

It is also possible to band material into low-, medium- and high-risk categories based upon the age of the material, together with risk-increasing factors such as whether the work was created with any commercial intent and the nature of the rights holder, as shown in Table 6.2 opposite.

Other recent approaches to risk management using a similar low-, medium- and high-risk approach include the Web2Rights Risk Management Calculator[4] and the risk assessor associated with digitising the Edwin Morgan Scrapbook (Stobo, Patterson and Deazley, 2017).

Acceptable use policies and procedures

Anyone using an organisation's information and communications technologies should be aware of and adhere to its acceptable use policy

---

3. See www.bmmagazine.co.uk/news/bentley-motors-ordered-to-small-independent-hundreds-of-thousands-in-brand-battle. At the time this chapter was written, Bentley Motors were thinking of appealing against the verdict.
4. https://web.archive.org/web/20150501144628/www.web2rights.com/OERIPRSupport/risk-management-calculator

Table 6.2 *Copyright infringement risk factors*

Item ID	Creation or publication date	Created with an initial intention to monetise and/or by re-known rights holders	Use without due diligence	Use with due diligence	Do not use
	LOW RISK Pre-1890	(This column is redundant for works of this period)	X		
	LOW RISK 1890–1990	NO	X		
	MEDIUM RISK 1890–1990	YES	X		
	MEDIUM RISK 1991–	NO	X		
	HIGH RISK 1991-	YES			X

(AUP). AUPs should make it clear that the organisation has legal responsibilities with regard to IPR and all users have to fulfil these responsibilities. AUPs should also make it clear what will happen if users fail to comply. The responsibilities may also be referred to in other relevant documents, such as staff codes of practice and agreements for members or users of library and information services. The provisions in AUPs should be backed up with procedures for identifying and investigating potential infringements. The procedures may form part of staff disciplinary procedures (as well as student disciplinary procedures in educational institutions). In public libraries, warnings may be issued or membership may be revoked in the case of breaches. In all the cases, the procedures for investigating and dealing with infringing behaviour should be communicated to users and should be followed closely.

Notice and take-down procedures

Organisations should develop procedures to deal with complaints from third parties about infringements of their IPR. These complaints could potentially include any aspect of IP, but libraries and information services are most likely to be concerned with allegations of infringement of copyright and related rights. Notice and take-down procedures apply when potential infringement is detected or notified. The infringing material could be hosted by the organisation, on an intranet or a web page for example, or accessed using the organisation's systems. There should be procedures in place to ensure that any material that is hosted or otherwise made available by LIK services is lawful. This should include checking that all requests to scan or copy in-copyright material for users comply with licence agreements and/or relevant copyright exceptions. Research and academic libraries should check publisher agreements for outputs submitted to institutional repositories and ensure that access complies with these agreements.

However, even with such procedures in place, organisations may still receive complaints and these should be investigated in a timely manner to reduce the likelihood of legal action and/or impact on reputation. Third parties should be directed to information on complaint procedures and provided with a means of submitting their complaint and supporting documentation. This could be achieved, for example, through the organisation's website. Contact details should be provided for the person or department responsible for dealing with IP-related complaints. If a complaint is received via another route, e.g., by post or by phone, it should be forwarded quickly to the appropriate recipient. This means that staff must be aware of what to do when complaints are received. Procedures from this point onwards will ensure that enough information has been received to investigate the complaint, the third party is notified that the complaint has been received and investigated, and relevant staff (for example in the IT department or external relations if necessary) within the organisation are notified as action may need to be taken to take down offending material temporarily or permanently, depending on the outcome of the investigation. Procedures should include setting timescales for actions to be taken: for example, how many working days it will take for material to be removed and for the outcome of investigations to be communicated to the complainant.

This process will reflect the organisation's approach to risk. A risk-averse organisation will take down the material immediately and may do so permanently even if the legitimacy of the complaint is questionable. The person responsible for the alleged infringement should be notified and provided with relevant information, such as the reasons for the decision made and disciplinary procedure if appropriate. Information about any appeals procedures should be communicated. There is, unlike in UK patent and registered trade mark law, no provision in UK copyright law to deter false claims of copyright infringement. For a library and information service, a policy of immediate and permanent take-down may raise ethical issues, as a policy of risk intolerance may have a chilling effect on the right to freedom of expression. A less risk-averse organisation will also have procedures in place to formulate challenges to complaints. This will require gathering information to support the challenge and then issuing a counter-complaint to the third party. The material in question would probably not be available during this process.

Table 6.3 sets out a sample take-down procedure.

Table 6.3 *Sample take-down procedure*	
Phase	**Timescale**
Phase 1: Receive objection, verify complaint and initially remove content	
Receive objection Notify copyright officer (if you have one) or a nominated member of staff and relevant curatorial/exhibitions staff depending upon the nature of the objection. Initially verify identity of complainant, nature of the complaint and the legitimacy of the complaint. If the objection is initially verified, notify staff responsible for websites/publishing/licensing, depending on the nature of the objection, and ensure the item is taken down immediately. *Acknowledge objection:* 'Dear X I am writing to acknowledge receipt of your complaint regarding content of an item in . . .. I have suspended access to the item pending verification of the complaint. In the event that I verify your complaint, I will comply fully with your request. I will endeavour to respond fully to your enquiry within one month, although this depends on the complexity of the investigation.'	Within seven working days of receipt of objection

Continued

Table 6.3 *Continued*	
Phase 2: Investigation of objection and determination of legal/rights status	
Co-ordinate investigation *Verify identity of complainant* In the case of material on your platform that has been deposited by a third party, contact depositor if necessary using the following template: *Write to depositor* 　Dear X 　Reference: [Item details] 　I am writing to advise you that the organisation has received a complaint regarding content that you deposited in [date]. The nature of the complaint is detailed below. On receipt of this complaint, the organisation suspended access to the material. 　Please respond to me regarding this complaint within 30 days of the date of this communication either accepting or refuting the complaint. If the latter, please provide an argument and supporting evidence that the alleged infringing material is legitimate. If you fail to respond to this communication within 30 days, the organisation will assume that you accept the complaint. [include information that identifies the material, the nature of the complaint, and the applicable law].	Up to 1 month after receipt of objection
Phase 3: Completion of investigation and updating records	
Decide outcome of the investigation, reinstating content if the complaint proves to be invalid. Inform the complainant. Record and document accurate rights information. Ensure that all staff using the material are aware of the confirmed rights status of the material and respond accordingly. Keep a record of the objection and response.	Within 1 working week after completion of Phase 2

Sample take-down notice

'In the event that you are the owner of the copyright in any of the material on this website and do not consent to the use of your material in accordance with the terms of conditions of use of this website, please contact us and we will withdraw your material from our website forthwith on receipt of your written objection and proof of ownership.'

Performances in libraries

Libraries might host public performances of copyright work on their premises. As performing, showing or playing of copyright works are restricted acts, it is likely that permission from the rights holder (or an appropriate licensing agency) is required unless copyright exceptions apply. Performance of live music or playing recorded music will require a licence from PPL PRS for Music[5] and showing films will require a licence from MPLC[6] or Filmbank[7] and PRS for Music. Singalongs for children will almost certainly require a PRS for Music licence. Public readings of brief extracts from in-copyright literary works are not considered to be copyright infringement, but problems will arise if the recitation is recorded in any way, or if the recitation covers a large proportion of the work. If the author reads their own work and they have retained the right to perform their work, then no other permission should be required. If libraries host public performances, they will have to develop procedures to ensure that no one infringes rights in copyright works or in the performance. These procedures should include informing audiences that they should not make recordings and definitely not make recordings publicly available. It may be challenging to prevent infringing behaviour during performances, so clear warnings should be given to audiences. It should be noted that video recording of such events may also have data protection implications if identifiable individuals are included in the recording.

---

5. https://pplprs.co.uk/themusiclicence
6. www.themplc.co.uk
7. www.filmbankmedia.com/licences

Top tips

1   Consider how you might mitigate risks when considering the use of third-party-owned works. These might include:

   (a) disclaimers

   (b) credit lines

   (c) notice and take-down policies and procedures

   (d) reproducing any images in low resolution

   (e) limiting use to low-risk works only (see below)

   (f) restricting any use to 'non-commercial research or private study' or 'criticism or review'

   (g) putting money aside in case rights holders come forward and/or taking out appropriate liability insurance, as discussed above.

2   Decide how many attempts you will make to try and trace rights holders. This should reflect your organisation's appetite for risk and the resources available to clear rights, as well as any legislative requirements if making use of any orphan works solutions.

3   Quick wins to finding rights holders include image-recognition sites such as Tin Eye Reverse Image Search,[8] as well as the WATCH File.[9]

4   Document your reasonable searches on a centrally accessible database so that you and your colleagues can refer to them at a later point.

5   Record the date of the searches and who carried them out so that you have a reference point if you need it!

6   Remember that whilst proportionality and making informed judgments is crucial, it is not an exact science.

7   If you are taking out the Orphan Works Licence or using the EU Orphan Works Exception, you may need to consider carrying out more extensive searches to qualify for either.

---

8. www.tineye.com
9. https://norman.hrc.utexas.edu/watch

7 Procedures: using and negotiating licences for access to information resources

Introduction

Whether you are providing access and usage rights to information resources (digital, print, and/or any other media or format) in which you own the rights (licensing out) or signing licences with organisations that are offering to supply electronic information to your institution (licensing in), negotiating the right terms will be extremely important. Contract management is an essential component of copyright compliance, an area of responsibility that has grown rapidly in recent years, and arguably one cannot do one's job as a manager of an electronic information service without getting involved in these crucial information law issues. Even if you work for an institution that has in-house lawyers, few, if any of them will have any experience of contractual terms within the context of LIK services, and specifically of contracts relating to access to information resources and/or information management issues. This chapter is written largely from the point of view of someone who is thinking of buying in from a third party offering a licence. If you are proposing to license out the use of resources that your institution holds the rights to, think of this chapter as identifying the issues you will have to address to satisfy potential clients of your services.

The electronic information industry

The electronic information industry (which term includes those selling – or offering for free – information over the web as well as through other electronic media) is a particularly complex industry. This is in terms of the players who are involved, the many relationships that are possible between these players, as well as the inevitability that the players will take on multiple roles in the supply chain of resources, depending upon your relationship to the information resources themselves. This complexity is one (but by no means the only) reason why it is so difficult to measure the size or growth rate of the industry. Who, then, are the players involved in the industry?

The first player in the electronic information industry is the *information provider*, also known as the *database producer* or similar terms. This is an individual or organisation that creates information, which is offered directly to end-users or which is licensed to other organisations (often called aggregators) who allow users access to them. Information providers can be, but are not always, also publishers in media other than electronic, e.g. print. They can be commercial organisations, learned societies, not-for-profit institutions, government departments, individuals, universities, and so on. Information providers usually own the copyright or database rights of the material on offer, but not always: for example, a newspaper or magazine publisher may only hold limited rights to material supplied to that publisher by freelance journalists. The volume of the information on offer can be large or small, static or constantly growing, updated in real time or at regular intervals such as daily or weekly. Many services used by the financial community are relatively small databases, mainly comprising numbers rather than words, being constantly updated with new information, such as share prices or exchange rates, overwriting the old information. In the library/information market, the norm is for the information on offer to be primarily words, to be steadily growing with an archive that is rarely, if ever, amended, and with daily, weekly or monthly updates of new materials. On the web, some sites are more or less static, whilst others change constantly by means of the addition of new web pages and/or by changes to existing pages.

The next player is the *aggregator,* in the past known as the *online host.* This organisation makes a number of information collections available to clients through its own computer services. It may own copyright and/or database rights in some, or all of the material on offer, but sometimes it does not own the information and must license it from whoever owns the rights. Users can access the aggregator's services through networks or the internet. Aggregators can be in the private sector, not-for-profit organisations, etc. A typical example is Science Direct, owned by Elsevier and offering the full text of Elsevier scholarly journals, together with abstracts from some non-Elsevier scholarly journals.

The next player is the *licensee*, such as the LIK manager, who typically is responsible both for negotiating the licences with those who provide electronic information services and for promoting the resulting services to their end-user community.

The final player is, of course, the *user*. Initially, most users of electronic information were trained intermediaries, typically librarians and information scientists. Nowadays, the majority are end-users.

The licences you will encounter

The subscriber contract is at the end of the contractual chain. The contract may be for occasional or irregular use, or may be a site licence arrangement between a major information provider (for example, a publisher such as John Wiley) and a large corporate purchaser. The subscriber contract is sometimes, but not always, negotiated between parties of equal strength. The information supplier may be stating, 'here is my contract, take it or leave it'. The subscriber is either not allowed to negotiate the terms, or is strongly discouraged from doing so. It would not be economic for the supplier to negotiate contractual terms individually with many organisations, each with their own interests and priorities. However, when large institutions sign deals, the electronic publisher needs that large institution, and the income it represents, as much as the institution needs the information. So, the larger the institution you work for, the more chance you have of negotiating changes to the supplier's standard contract. This is even more the case when an organisation (such as Jisc) is negotiating on behalf of an entire country's set of organisations.

There are basically three types of licences an electronic information manager will encounter. These are: *shrink-wrap, click-through* and *negotiated*. *Shrink-wrap* is typically found with CDs, DVDs and software. By tearing open the package you agree to the terms and conditions imposed on you. If you cannot read the terms and conditions before ripping it open, and you don't like what you see when you do, you are entitled in law to return the item to the supplier and to get your money back.[1] These licences are, however, non-negotiable. So if you don't return the software, you are bound by the terms and conditions imposed on you unless they are trying

---

1. Consumer Rights Act 2015.

to impose terms and conditions upon you which take away 'rights' provided to you under, for example, certain exceptions to copyright.

Click-through licences are very common on the web. Many people click on the 'I agree' button without looking at the terms and conditions properly. By doing so, the person cannot complain if they subsequently discover they have agreed to something they hadn't intended to. We suspect, for example, that most individuals do not bother to check the terms and conditions of social media sites, such as Twitter, that they connect to. Such sites often state that by using the site, you agree that the site owner can reproduce and/or sub-license anything you post to any third party.

As noted earlier, a lot of *negotiated licences* are not negotiable unless you work for a large institution, or your institution is part of a consortium, which negotiates with the information supplier. Even if you can negotiate on details, a problem remains. You negotiate each one separately with a different supplier, and so, as a result, will have a series of contracts with subtly different terms and conditions. This, in turn means that you must inform the users in your institution about these different terms and conditions. It's confusing and frustrating for you, and for your users. Not all licences involve payment of licence fees. Thus, the CC suite of licences are a set of (in practice non-negotiable) licences, but they have one thing in common; if you sign up to a service offering one, no fees are payable.

What is more, most licence agreements typically last three or four years, and then you have to renegotiate, so there will be regular changes to those terms and conditions as well. Despite all this, it is not all gloom and doom. LIK managers have some resources to help them fight this confusing situation.

The first is the development of consortia, and the second is the publication of statements of licensing principles. Anti-cartel laws mean that electronic publishers are not allowed to work together when setting licence terms and conditions, and prices. However, they do not stop LIK services working together to create a unified purchasing institution. Consortia deals are common in the education sector. For example, in the UK higher education sector, Jisc Collections will often negotiate a deal with an electronic information supplier on behalf of the community, and Universities UK and the Guild of Higher Education negotiate with the Copyright Licensing Agency (CLA) for photocopying and scanning licences for the entire sector. There are basically two types of consortia deal. In the first, once the consortium has agreed the terms with the seller then all the consortium members are obliged to sign up. In the second, once the consortium has agreed the terms, it shows them to individual members who may or may not choose to sign up. Obviously, the electronic information industry prefers the former.

Finally, there are statements of licensing principles. These are statements issued by groups of LIK managers, or their professional bodies, regarding the minimum terms they expect from licences. They also note the terms they regard as unacceptable (for example, prices that are far higher than the equivalent print product, or contracts where the supplier reserves the right to increase prices without notice). They strongly advise LIK managers *not* to sign up to any deal that does not conform to these principles, but of course, anyone can sign any deal they wish. Such statements are often complemented by model contractual clauses, such as those published by Jisc.[2] The suggestion here is that the librarian or information manager, rather than receiving the draft licence from the supplier (as is usual) and negotiating on it, says 'oh no, I want you to follow MY licence' and presents a model licence back to the supplier. In some cases, publishers have participated in the development of such licences. This gives them a stamp of authority, which makes it hard for an electronic information provider to refuse to use it. Another great advantage of using a standard licence is that, as the name implies, you get standardisation, so the end-users of the electronic information know, for example, that whatever the source of the information, they are always allowed to download and print. Standard licences can help reduce negotiation time, and can be used to compare with a licence you have been offered to evaluate it.

What's in a typical licence?

The licence is a document that can range from one to hundreds of pages long. Typically, the licence agreement will cover the following issues (though not, of course, necessarily in this order):

- ◆ parties
- ◆ definitions
- ◆ obligations on the licensor (the supplier of the information)
- ◆ term – how long the licence lasts for
- ◆ how the licence gets renewed

---

2. www.jisc-collections.ac.uk/Support/How-Model-Licences-work

◆ fees payable
◆ conditions of use of the information
◆ authorised users
◆ limitations of liabilities, waivers and disclaimers
◆ grounds for terminating early
◆ governing law
◆ dispute resolution
◆ 'complete agreement'
◆ support and documentation provided
◆ confidentiality
◆ other clauses.

Parties

This simply confirms who is entering into the contract – typically, the LIK manager's employer, and the supplier of the electronic information.

Definitions

This section defines the electronic information that will be supplied. Special jargon used in the contract, such as 'authorised users' or 'secure network', might also be defined here.

Obligations on the licensor

There may be an obligation to inform subscribers of changes to content or prices, and perhaps an obligation to provide user manuals, help desk, training, etc. Almost *never* will you find a guarantee to maintain high-quality information or to guarantee the number or amount of updates per year.

Term

This says how long the licence contract lasts for. Typically, a licence agreement lasts for two to four years from date of signature.

Renewal

There are two schools of thought here. The first is that coming up towards the due date for the contract to expire, the parties have to get together and negotiate a brand-new licence agreement. The second is that the contract automatically renews for a further period of time, and so on *ad infinitum,* unless either party tells the other that it does not wish to renew. If either party happens not to like particular aspects of the contract any more, it tells the other it does not wish to renew the existing contract, but is interested in a renegotiation.

Fees

This states how much the client has to pay for the licence. There may be an obligation on the subscriber to pay their bills promptly. There may be remarks about interest payable if the client pays late. There may be remarks about VAT, sales tax or other taxes to be paid as well. The provider of information often reserves the right to raise (or lower!) its prices, though automatic price rises linked to inflation should be resisted if they are not accompanied by improved terms, e.g., increased repertoire, or increased flexibility on what users can do with the licensed materials.

Contracts often provide for 'reasonable' (e.g. three months') notice of any such changes, or a promise that changes will take place no more often than once a year, and permit the subscriber to cancel the contract upon receipt of notice of such changes (or changes to content).

Conditions of use

This is a crucial part of the licence. It is the part that states what can and cannot be done with the information. If the licence is silent on any particular point of use, then copyright law takes over, and a user can only do what exceptions to copyright allow. There may well be restrictions on downloading, re-dissemination, passing retrieved materials outside the institution, systematic copying, reselling of output, etc. There may be other special terms. These may include copyright notices that must appear on each item viewed, printed or downloaded, a requirement to report on numbers of items downloaded, or a maximum time period for which items can be downloaded. There may be a right for the supplier to visit to inspect for verification purposes. The question of distribution to intranets and portals is important. Clients receive data and send it to a number of terminals within their institution, which may be widely scattered on one or several sites. Some recent agreements with Elsevier have included terms regarding the company's right to access metadata (such as names and numbers of users, search terms employed, etc.) regarding the use of its services. Such requirements will have data protection implications.

Authorised users

Only authorised users can access the information. Such users need to be defined, and this is not always easy. Consider an institution that is on many sites, perhaps in one country, perhaps in many. How does one define the site in such cases? Can anyone on any site access the information, or must they be on one particular site to do so? What about employees who are away from site? Can they log in remotely and gain access to the information? All these points need to be addressed to both parties' satisfaction. They also have to address, in the case of universities, the rights of distance-learning and part-time students, and visitors who are not staff or students, to make use of the materials.

Limitations of liability, waivers and disclaimers

Users of electronic information services can experience quality problems at various levels. First, there is the information itself. Then there are the system's search and retrieval features. Documentation, charging and billing procedures, and help facilities for customers, are important. Failure or errors can occur at any stage, and indeed sometimes it is difficult to know who is at fault.

The most obvious issue for users of information services is that of the content. Problems can include typographical errors, misspellings, gaps in coverage and indexing errors. When spelling errors occur in important record fields, or citations are inaccurate, retrieval can be significantly affected. This is a particularly serious problem in the areas of financial, legal, patent, climate change or medical information, when key decisions might be being made on the basis of the information retrieved. Timeliness is also often an important issue for searchers. Of course, different criteria are important to different searchers, and even the same searcher will have different quality criteria in mind at different times, depending on the nature of the search. Information providers know that quality in electronic information services is an important issue. However, often the opinion of a particular information provider on what is high quality or not can differ from that of its customers.

What if the information is inaccurate – the raw data is wrong, the wording of the text is misleading, the indexing terms are inappropriate, the data is out of date, or incomplete, or the information is defamatory, infringes someone's copyright, or is illegal in some other way? What if the information retrieval software leads to corruption or loss of data or inaccurate searches? Erroneous information rarely causes direct physical injury to humans or material damage to structures. But it does sometimes. For example, a medical resource may give incorrect drug dosages or a database on chemicals may mislead about toxicity and acceptable exposure limits or perhaps on the risks of explosion. Likewise a mechanical or electrical engineering database may provide misleading instructions, which result in the collapse of a structure, or a person being electrocuted. Erroneous information can lead to financial loss. Thus, a credit rating may be inaccurate; as a result, the searcher does business with a company they thought was financially sound when it was not. The company collapses and the searcher's employer loses money. Alternatively, the incorrect information might indicate that the third party has a poor credit rating, and as a result, the third party loses business. Of course, if a service offers an incorrect credit rating about an individual, data protection law may well kick in. If a company has an incorrect credit rating, there might be a case for a libel action, but that is a topic that is outside the remit of this book. Other examples could arise from incorrect exchange rates leading to losses in the markets, or inaccurate reporting about a company may result in a decline in share price and thereby a personal loss for shareholders. Another example might be a company that is planning to manufacture a product carries out a patent search, finds no relevant patents, proceeds to build the plant, then finds it is indeed infringing a patent and is sued for substantial sums. 100% perfect information resources are impossible to achieve. The key question for an information supplier is how to achieve sufficient high-quality coverage to obtain a competitive edge without excessive expense.

Courts around the world have been willing to compensate for direct loss by the individual or company, but are reluctant to cover consequential loss (such as the shareholders in the above example). They are also reluctant to award damages if the searcher relied too heavily on a single information resource when they should have used more than one source; in other words, the searcher must use reasonable skill and judgement in doing the search and evaluating the results. Information suppliers are understandably nervous of being sued for inaccuracies. To cover themselves, they will almost certainly put a waiver clause in the licence agreement, and will take out suitable liability insurance.

Although waiver clauses are common, and licensees sign them without too much thought, it has to be said that there is some doubt about their validity in law. A database producer must be expected to show a certain standard of care and expertise. If the information provider was reckless or negligent in its behaviour, it might be liable irrespective of waiver clauses they inserted into the agreement. A court would probably regard a total exoneration of liability in the examples quoted above as 'unfair'. The courts would almost certainly decide that one couldn't provide any type of commercial service without accepting some responsibility for it. So although disclaimers, or waivers of liability, are to be found in all licence agreements, they don't necessarily mean the licensee is left without any possibility of compensation if the licensor has made serious mistakes with its content or search software.

In any case, in the UK and in some other countries, one cannot exclude one's liability for damage caused by gross negligence, and any clauses to that effect are invalid. Quite often this is addressed in the clauses by the key words 'to the extent permitted by law, we waive liability . . .'.

Some suppliers put a maximum (say the cost of the annual subscription) on any damages they may have to pay in a liability case; or they may say the subscriber is entitled to terminate if they find errors. A clause in the licence agreement along the lines of:

> Producer shall use its best efforts to maintain a high quality database, this quality to be measured by accuracy, currency and exhaustivity as reflected in the contents list contained in Appendix . . .. Producer shall use all reasonable precautions to avoid any form of error in the contents of the database, including errors in indexing terms and coding.

would at least show consciousness of the need for care.

Termination

The information provider will invariably be given the right to terminate if the subscriber is in material breach of the contract. Similarly, the subscriber may be given the right to terminate upon notice of change of content or prices.

Applicable law

This is a statement of which country's law under which the contract will be interpreted. Since the subscriber has to probably take the contract as they find it, complete with waivers and exclusions of liability, it is important to know under which country's law the contract will be considered if a question of fairness arises. Typically, the provider uses the law of the country where its head office is situated.

Dispute resolution

There may be a clause allowing for independent arbitration in the case of disputes.

Complete agreement

There may be a clause confirming that this licence agreement represents the complete agreement between the parties. This means that any letters, memos, e-mails, etc., relevant to the agreement and exchanged either before, or after signature, do not form part of the agreement.

Support and documentation

The supplier should agree to offer a help desk, provide training, documentation, and so on. There may or may not be charges for some of these services.

Assignment

Each party often agrees that it cannot assign the licence to someone else without the express agreement of the other party. There may be special provisions relating to this if one or other of the parties is acquired by, or merges with, another organisation during the term of the agreement.

Confidentiality

This states that the contents of the licence shall be kept confidential. This can have a seriously inhibiting effect on discussions between a prospective licensee and colleagues in other organisations, as people wanting help on particular contracts they are negotiating might not be able to quote directly from the clauses that cause them concern. Obviously suppliers are keen that details of clauses and of prices do not leak out, as this would give competitive advantage to both buyers of electronic information, and to the supplier's competitors.

Other clauses

There will be one on *force majeure*, which states that neither party is liable if due to circumstances genuinely beyond their control they cannot fulfil their side of the bargain. There is likely to be a requirement that the client keeps all passwords confidential and/or immediately informs the supplier if it suspects any password has been disclosed to an unauthorised third party.

There should ideally be a clause explicitly stating that nothing in the agreement shall prevent a user from carrying out any acts that are permitted under an exception to copyright. In the UK, as noted earlier, recent changes to copyright law mean that anyone in theory can download materials from an electronic information service they have legitimate access to for the purposes of non-commercial text and data mining.[3] However, the licensor is also permitted under this amended law to implement measures to prevent overload of their systems by such activities, and many service providers have taken advantage of this to install TPMs that prevent large-scale downloading. This is a controversial area, and if any of the staff of the licensee are likely to want to make use of text and data mining, there should be a negotiated clause in the agreement explicitly covering this issue.

Top tips when negotiating licences presented to you by third parties

1   Understand, before you start negotiating, how you wish to use the digital resources, who you want to access them, how much you can afford to spend and how long you want to commit to.
2   Read the small print of the contract: the devil is in the detail.
3   Use your size, number of users, etc., to negotiate the best possible deal for your employer in terms of, for example, who are the authorised users and what are the permitted uses, as well as the

---

3. As noted elsewhere, at the time this book was written the European Union was considering introducing such an exception as well.

licence fee. Can you negotiate the best terms as a group of organisations and/or find a way to reduce costs all round and seek a licence that covers you all?

4   Take into account any hidden extras, such as the administration of the licence, compliance requirements, etc., when assessing the value and cost of the licence.

5   Find out what format the digital resources will be delivered in and whether there are any TPMs associated with the service, which might preclude you from benefitting from the exceptions to copyright; for example the discussion on text and data mining above.

6   If you are unhappy with any of the terms and conditions, for example the costs, or if the licensor wishes to have access to personal data about users of its service, conflicting with your data protection compliance obligations:
    ◆   go back and re-negotiate
    ◆   check for alternative sources of the same or similar information, assessing their coverage, quality and price and how they match the needs of your users
    ◆   if need be, don't sign the licence.

7   Don't sign a licence that:
    ◆   doesn't clearly define authorised users, uses and other important components to your satisfaction
    ◆   is ambiguous in any of its wording
    ◆   uses contract law to override your institution's ability to benefit fully from the copyright exceptions; although many copyright exceptions include provisions that prevent this from happening, not all do
    ◆   doesn't include a warranty from the licensor that it either owns, or has an appropriate licence for the content offered, and an indemnity clause against any claims from third parties that the licensee has used infringing materials, so that the licensee does not have to pay damages in such cases
    ◆   doesn't deal suitably with data protection, including not dealing with letting you know if there has been a data breach which has resulted in individual users' details, including perhaps their search histories, reaching unauthorised third parties, or taking too long to let you know about the breach
    ◆   has a non-cancellation clause

◆ has clauses with ambiguous wording, e.g., concerning periods of time, or relating to costs for usage.

8 Regularly review your suite of licences to ensure each one represents value for money, fulfils the needs of your users and remains fit for purpose.

9 Learn about negotiation skills! There are many excellent books and courses to give advice on this subject.

Further reading

Durrant, F. (2006) *Negotiating Licences for Digital Resources*, Facet Publishing, is a bit dated, but is very approachable.

Harris, L. E. (2018) *Licensing Digital Content*, 3rd edn, American Library Association, is up to date and based on US law.

Williams, A., Calow, D. and Lee, A. (2011) *Digital Media Contracts*, Oxford University Press.

All three of these books cover clauses to look out for as well as negotiation skills.

Owen, L. (2018) *Clark's Publishing Agreements*, 10th edn, Bloomsbury is *the* standard work for model agreements, including those discussed in this chapter, but is an expensive reference work. It does not cover negotiation skills.

Procedures: data protection and freedom of information

Introduction

Organisations in the UK must handle personal data in accordance with the provisions of the General Data Protection Regulation (GDPR), which is embodied in the Data Protection Act 2018. The Act ensures that the GDPR principles will remain in force if and when the UK leaves the EU.[1] Organisations collect and process personal data about staff and individuals who interact with the organisation in some way, including customers, users, partners, contractors and visitors. LIK services also handle personal data and therefore must comply with data protection law. LIK services will hold personnel records, user and borrowing records, catalogue records about living individuals and possibly archives containing personal data. Research data repositories may also contain personal data.

Processing of personal data must be carried out in accordance with the data protection principles. These principles are: lawfulness, fairness and transparency; purpose limitation; data minimisation; accuracy; storage limitation; integrity and confidentiality and accountability (General Data Protection Regulation, art. 5). Some of the data processed by libraries will be sensitive in nature, that is, special category data under data protection law (General Data Protection Regulation, art. 9(1)). For example, health libraries or libraries in institutions where medical research is carried out may process several types of special category data, including health; race; ethnic origin; genetics; sex life or sexual orientation. Additional conditions must be fulfilled to process this category of data to make it lawful. Children are also afforded specific attention under the GDPR (recital 38), which is relevant to school, college and public libraries in particular.

---

1. At the time of writing (November 2019), the status regarding Brexit is still uncertain.

Data protection law allows archiving of personal data for certain purposes and data sharing for research purposes in certain circumstances. This is possible because of exemptions to some of the data protection principles that govern the processing of personal data. The principles that are particularly relevant to archiving personal data and making it available for research purposes are purpose limitation and storage limitation. There are circumstances where further processing for archival and research purposes is lawful, for example in the case of research data where the data subjects have consented to this storage and further processing. In other circumstances, processing must conform to the requirements of the relevant exceptions and this has implications for procedures.

The GDPR specifies that further processing can be carried out for 'archiving purposes in the public interest, scientific or historical research or statistical purposes' (art. 5(1)(b)) and that personal data may be stored for longer periods if it will be 'processed solely for archiving purposes in the public interest, scientific or historical research purposes or statistical purposes' subject' (art. 5(1)(e)). 'Scientific' here should be interpreted broadly, and should be considered to cover any field of study. Both of these exceptions are conditional upon the processing being compatible with art. 89(1), which says that where possible the data should be anonymised or pseudonymised to respect the principle of data minimisation. This would be appropriate for research using anonymised and/or aggregated data. It may require datasets to be anonymised, which may be relatively straight-forward for quantitative data but more challenging for qualitative data.

Anonymisation would be a serious impediment to certain types of historical research and biographical studies. However, as stated in the UK's Data Protection Act 2018 (schedule 2, pt 6), certain GDPR provisions do not apply if they would 'prevent or seriously impair the achievement' of scientific and historical research or statistical purposes. The GDPR leaves open the possibility of processing personal data for archival and research purposes if those purposes would be frustrated by anonymising data. However, there is a provision that the art. 89(1) requirement that appropriate safeguards should be in place to protect the data subject if the processing of personal data is 'likely to cause substantial damage or substantial distress to a data subject.' Data protection law does not necessarily prevent access to personal data in archives for researchers, but it does recognise the need for a balance between protecting the rights and freedoms of data subjects and archival and research purposes. Organisations, including LIK services must undertake risk assessments and develop access procedures based on the outcomes of these assessments.

Data protection policies need to set out the organisation's overall approach to compliance with the data protection principles, including the role and responsibilities of the person responsible for data protection matters. Organisations must also develop data protection procedures, registers, repositories, archives, impact assessments, appraisal and retention procedures and schedules. Procedures should also include how and when all of these are updated, how all personnel and other individuals involved with the organisation will be trained to recognise and handle personal data, requests and complaints responsibly and how overall awareness of the importance of data protection will be maintained.

Practical implementation of the law for library, information and knowledge workers

There are a number of practical steps organisations should undertake. These can be broken down into four steps – gap analysis, risk analysis, project planning and implementation (Voigt and von dem Bussche, 2017).

The first stage is to analyse existing data protection practice in the organisation and identify the gaps that need to be filled to fulfil the revised law. The second stage is to assess the risks in the current gaps as regards, e.g. the sensitivity of the personal data being held, and what activities are most prone to risk. Based on these first two, an organisation-wide project plan to address the high-risk gaps should be developed and costed and it should divide things into short-term urgent changes and longer-term less urgent but necessary changes. Finally, of course, the plan must be implemented. This should include awareness-developing programmes for all relevant staff, possibly also developing a data protection management system, and quite probably appointing a data protection officer (DPO). Each organisation should assess its own processing to decide if it needs to appoint such an expert, ideally by means of an information audit and privacy impact assessment. There will probably also have to be new or improved record keeping of data protection-relevant activities. Procedures must also be put in place to monitor data protection standards and, where necessary, to implement changes to the organisation's personal data processing activities. Finally, the new obligation to report significant data protection breaches must be understood and put into effect throughout the organisation. All this implies significant costs and effort for many organisations, including of course, LIK units. For that reason, buy-in from top management is essential. It is perfectly possible and, arguably, desirable, if the unit wishes, for the library or information unit within an organisation to become the centre of expertise in data protection matters for the organisation.

Data protection officers (DPOs)

Organisations must decide whether they will appoint a DPO. Public authorities or bodies (Data Protection Act 2018, s. 7) are required to do so. Therefore public, educational, NHS, national, government, parliamentary and other public-sector library and archive services should have a dedicated DPO, or a DPO appointed by their public authority. Some non-public-sector organisations must also appoint a DPO if their core or primary business activities 'require the regular and systematic monitoring of individuals on a large scale' or 'processing on a large scale of special category data, or data relating to criminal convictions and offences' (Information Commissioner's Office, 2019). This is unlikely to be the case for most library and information services.

Chapter 2 introduced the new GDPR requirements for the appointment of DPOs in organisations; such officers might work for data processors rather than data controllers. Their duties will include:

- ◆ monitoring compliance with the law
- ◆ assisting in the development of data protection impact assessments
- ◆ acting as a data protection contact point
- ◆ keeping records of data protection-relevant operations
- ◆ understanding the risks involved in activities within their remit
- ◆ responsibility for registration with their national data protection authority, such as the UK ICO.

Ideally, they should have knowledge of the business sector and of the organisation of the controller. They should also be required to keep up to date on significant legal cases of relevance, and on guidance issued by their data protection authority. Membership of relevant professional data protection associations should also be encouraged.

Documenting processing activities

Documenting processing activities makes sense, as this helps organisations ensure that they meet their obligations under data protection law as well as supporting good information governance more generally. The GDPR includes documentation requirements in art. 30(1) for controllers, and art 30(2) for processors. The documentation requirements are more onerous for organisations with 250 or more employees. For these organisations, the following should be documented:

◆ the name and contact details of the organisation, including the DPO if applicable
◆ the purposes for which personal data is processed
◆ the categories of individuals and personal data processed
◆ the categories of recipients of any personal data sharing
◆ details of data transfers to third countries, and the safeguards in place for such transfers
◆ data retention schedules
◆ technical and organisational security measures.

This information can be combined with information about data subjects' rights in privacy notices. These notices should be made available via websites and other appropriate means whenever data is collected. Further information that should be documented includes:

◆ the lawful basis for the processing; this may or may not include consent
◆ details of any automated decision making
◆ the sources of personal data.

The design of privacy notices should be carefully considered, as it may be appropriate to create layered notices or to use suitable icons to make it easier for individuals to read and understand the information.

If the lawful basis for processing is consent, records should be kept to provide evidence that this consent meets the standard set out in the GDPR. Records should include the details of how consent was obtained and separate consents should be obtained for separate purposes so that it can be shown that consent is clear and specific. Requests for consent should also make it clear which third parties will be relying on the consent.

Procedures should also involve reviewing consent practices as and when anything changes. Procedures should be put in place to ensure that all records and documentation is kept up to date, so that it remains accurate. This includes privacy notices.

Data breaches

Personal data breaches can include:

◆ access by an unauthorised third party through their direct action or lax internal security procedures or practices
◆ deliberate or accidental action or inaction by a member of staff
◆ sending personal data to an incorrect recipient, e.g. wrong copy recipients to an e-mail
◆ USB stick, laptop or phone containing personal data being lost or stolen
◆ alteration of personal data without permission
◆ loss of availability of personal data.

When a security incident takes place, it must be established whether:

◆ a personal data breach has occurred
◆ the nature of that breach
◆ the steps to be taken in response to the breach.

Any data breaches should be documented. Not all breaches have to be reported to the ICO, but recording pertinent information on breaches supports the general requirement to implement effective technical and security measures. More serious breaches must be reported to the ICO, so procedures should be in place to identify and record the details and impact of any serious breaches that occur as quickly as possible. Organisations can then identify whether the breach is notifiable and meet the requirement of notification to the ICO within 72 hours. The GDPR also requires that where there have been breaches that pose a high risk to the affected individuals, those individuals must be notified quickly.

Data protection impact assessments

LIK workers may need to carry out data protection impact assessments (DPIAs) before embarking on new projects or introducing new services. DPIAs are used when a proposed project potentially poses high data-protection risks. The purpose of the DPIA is to identify risks and ways of reducing them. The assessment should describe the proposed processing, including scope, context and purposes. It should then consider whether the processing is necessary and proportional and what measures would be in place to ensure legal compliance. The risks to data subjects should then be identified and assessed and consideration should be given to whether further measures should be employed to reduce the risks.

The Information Commissioner's Office recommends that DPIAs should be carried out when any of the following are involved:

◆ evaluation or scoring
◆ automated decision making with significant effects
◆ systematic monitoring, processing of sensitive data or data of a highly personal nature
◆ processing on a large scale, processing of data concerning vulnerable data subjects
◆ innovative technological or organisational solutions
◆ processing that involves preventing data subjects from exercising a right or using a service or contract.

You should consider the potential impact of external aspects of service provision, for example internet service providers, information service suppliers or app stores.

You must do a DPIA for processing that is likely to result in a high risk to individuals. This includes some specified types of processing. You can use the checklist below to help you decide how to do a DPIA. It is also good practice to do a DPIA for any other major project that requires the processing of personal data.

Checklist for a DPIA

A DPIA should incorporate the following steps:

◆ describe the nature, scope, context and purposes of the processing

◆ identify the need for a DPIA
◆ assess necessity, proportionality and compliance measures
◆ describe the information flows
◆ identify the privacy and assess the risks to individuals
◆ identify any additional measures to mitigate those risks
◆ consult with internal and external stakeholders as needed throughout the process.

Responding to requests and complaints

The GDPR provides individuals with a set of rights in their personal data, and organisations, including LIK services, should be able to quickly identify and deal with data protection requests. This means that all staff should be sufficiently trained to know what to do with any requests and/or complaints that they become aware of. LIK services within larger organisations could designate a member of staff as data protection contact point or champion, and self-standing services could designate departmental data protection contacts. These local contact points could support colleagues in their day-to-day work and act as channels to pass requests and complaints to the DPO (if there is one) where appropriate.

As discussed in Chapter 2, data subjects have a number of rights. The right to be informed can be supported by privacy policies and active communication with individuals. However, procedures should be in place to allow individuals to easily make requests and complaints and to provide appropriate and sufficient supporting information. Communications should be acknowledged in a timely fashion. Unless a subject access request is particularly complex, a response should then be provided within a month of receiving the request. There should be robust procedures in place to consider requests and complaints, make appropriate responses, review responses if required and provide information to individuals on what to do if they are unhappy with the outcome of the process.

There should be a system in place to carry out relevant data processing changes as soon as possible after decisions that require them are reached. This could be updating, amending or deleting data. It could mean ceasing some aspects of processing altogether, or ensuring that data can be provided to data subjects in appropriate formats. Good data governance, clear lines of communication between relevant staff and functions and step-by-step procedures and will greatly facilitate the ability of organisations to comply with the law.

Data subject rights: a summary of what they are and what your organisation must do in response

◆ right to be informed – communicate clearly and use plain language in all your organisation's responses to SARs

◆ right of access – have in place processes to respond to SARs for what information you are holding

◆ right to rectification – ensure you correct inaccurate information in the data you are processing without delay

◆ right to erasure – you may be required to delete the data and stop processing it or publishing it (often called the right to be forgotten)

◆ right to restrict processing – where the accuracy or lawful processing is challenged, then systems are in place to ensure that temporary limits on the processing are imposed if required

◆ right to data portability – you may be asked to provide the personal data you hold, securely and in a machine-readable format, so it can be moved, copied or transferred to be used across different services

◆ right to object – ensure you have the right consents in place for activity such as direct marketing

◆ rights related to automated decision making – if there is additional profiling based on the data you hold, then an individual can object, and again, suitable systems must be in place to implement such requests.

Example procedure for responding to a subject access request

1   **Check the SAR is valid**

SARs can be verbal, in writing, on a form or in a letter or e-mail. If you receive an oral request, then ask that it is put in writing and/or direct the requester to an appropriate request form. As a general rule, do not share the personal data of anyone without their consent. Be aware that providing personal details of others can leave them open to fraud or impersonation. If you have any doubts about what you are being asked to do, then ask for the request in writing and forward it to the Data Protection Officer to co-ordinate. Take care to anonymise or redact any references to others that could identify them. If in doubt then check with the Privacy or Data Protection Officer and explain what you have done to the requester.

2 **Forward to the Data Protection Officer for co-ordination of the SAR**
SARs are co-ordinated by the DPO so forward any you receive to them at [e-mail address].

If you have a query or are unclear on the process or the handling then do look at the policy or ask the DPO.

3 **Check entitlement to the personal data**
Before you provide the personal data, you must be satisfied that the person is entitled to it. There are two parts to checking this entitlement:

3.1 *Check the identity of the person*
This check is to make sure that the person is really who they say they are.

Check identity using one or more of any of the following:
◆ passport
◆ driving licence
◆ birth certificate
◆ utility bill from last 3 months
◆ current vehicle registration document
◆ bank statement from last 3 months
◆ rent book from last 3 months

If an alternative is offered do check with the Privacy Officer as to whether this is an acceptable substitute.

Copies are acceptable, but we do prefer to see originals. Keep a copy on file as part of the record of processing the SAR and remember to return the originals to the requester using recorded delivery.

3.2 *Check the person is the same as the data subject*
This is important so that you do not disclose personal data to the wrong person. That would be a data breach and has serious consequences in data protection law. You need to complete this check even if you think you know the person, e.g. he or she is a colleague or a regular business contact. To check that they are the same individual as the one you hold personal data about, use that personal data to ask questions which only that individual could answer. It is the same as being asked your date of birth or the first line of your address when you are talking to your bank.

4   **Ensure all SARs on behalf of a person are genuine**

If someone is claiming to act on behalf of the data subject, do not provide data to them unless they have written authorisation signed by the data subject and evidence that it is genuine, e.g. proof of their relationship to the data subject.

Carry out the entitlement checks set out in 3.1 above.

5   **Responding to the SAR**

The deadline under the legislation is without delay and at the latest within one month of receipt of the SAR, i.e. 20 working days. This time starts to run from when you have the evidence needed about the requester's identity and can check that the request is valid. For complex or numerous requests, this period can be extended by a further two months. If the request is complex, then you will acknowledge the request within that first month and seek further clarification direct with the requester. Identifying precisely what information they want may well save you time. You can also explain why the extra time is needed. Where requests are vexatious or excessive, in particular because they are repetitive, then a reasonable administrative fee can be charged, or we may choose not to respond. In all cases, we must explain what is happening and give them the opportunity to clarify or resolve the issue. It is important to make it clear that we are handling the request under the Data Protection Act 2018 and also explain the right of redress to the Information Commissioner if they are dissatisfied and we have been unable to resolve their complaint.

Do use consistent and standardised wording when putting the response together.

As far as possible do meet the requester's requirements for format and method of sending the data. If the request is made by e-mail then we can provide the information by e-mail if the requester indicates this would be acceptable. It is important that you organise the material so that the applicant can make sense of it. Simply sending a batch of copies of e-mails is very often not helpful. At all stages of the assessment of each SAR, take care to document your decisions and approach as that may be relevant to support your assessment if it is challenged or queried in a subsequent complaint.

6   **Staff access to their data**

Special arrangements apply to requests by staff for personal data held about them, including their personnel records and references written about them.[2] These are handled by HR [or as appropriate]. Once validated, the request is passed to [the Data Protection Officer] so it can be handled centrally.

Freedom of information

FoI law applies to public authorities, so public sector LIK services, including public, state school, university, NHS and government libraries must comply with the law.[3] Information audits facilitate compliance, as public authorities must know what information they have so that they can fulfil their obligation to either publish information proactively or provide it when requested by members of the public. FoI assumes that everyone has the right to information, so the default position is that it should be provided. All requesters should be treated equally, unless there is evidence that a request is vexatious. In addition, UK FoI laws provide a number of exceptions that allow a public authority to refuse to disclose information.

FoI legislation covers all recorded information, so public authorities should be prepared to disclose written documents and e-mails, recorded voice conversations and CCTV recordings. Information received by public authorities (other than personal data) and document metadata (such as date of creation or e-mail headers) are also covered. The law includes provision of factual information held as datasets (Freedom of Information Act 2000, s. 11) and the ICO provides guidance for practice on releasing datasets for reuse (Information Commissioner's Office, 2015). The law covers information held by a public authority even if it is stored off-site or is held on the authority's behalf by another entity. Although FoI legislation requires public authorities to provide information, this does not extend to personal data, as discussed in Chapter 3.

Publication schemes

Public authorities must draw up a publication scheme and proactively publish both the scheme and the information listed in the scheme. The

---

2. The rules about references are discussed in Chapter 3.
3. Lists of public authorities can be found in the Freedom of Information Act 2000, www.legislation.gov.uk/ukpga/2000/36/schedule/1, and in the Freedom of Information (Scotland) Act 2002, www.legislation.gov.uk/asp/2002/13/contents, and is discussed further in Chapters 3 and 4.

publication scheme should list categories of information to be published, including policies and procedures, annual and financial reports. More formal information should be published but it is not compulsory to proactively publish other types of information, including unredacted minutes of meetings or archived records. Public authorities should use the appropriate ICO model publication scheme,[4] which is discussed in Chapter 9. Public authorities should also provide guidance on how the information is made available and details of any fees that will be charged. The ICO considers it reasonable to charge a fee to cover the costs of providing information, but does not consider it reasonable to charge for information published online (Information Commissioner's Office, 2019).

The benefit of drawing up a publication scheme is that staff can be made aware of its contents and quickly point members of the public to the published information if a request is made for it. Procedures should be put in place to ensure that new information is published as quickly as possible and the publication schedule is kept up to date. There should be a process in place to ensure that members of staff are aware of FoI publication commitments. Systems should be in place for the notification and publication of new information. The authority's website would be a suitable place to publish the scheme and information. If it is not possible to publish all the information online because of its format or physical state, arrangements should be put in place to let the public know why and provide contact details of who is responsible for the material and arranging access to it.

Recognising and responding to FoI requests

FoI requests can be received at any contact point in an organisation, including a library or information service. So all staff should know how to recognise such requests and what to do with them. The Information Commissioner's Office (2014) provides guidance on what information can be requested. Library, information and knowledge services may also be required to provide information to fulfil a request wherever it originated in the organisation; this is especially true if the service has any responsibilities for records, archives, information or data management. As with personal data, staff should be trained to understand the purpose of

---

4. https://ico.org.uk/for-organisations/guide-to-freedom-of-information/publication-scheme

FoI and the obligations under the law. Guidance should ideally be included at induction, in staff handbooks and perhaps also tested and certified through learning resources. Routine requests for information about services can be treated as such and answered directly. If the request cannot be answered directly, or if the enquirer refers to FoI legislation, then the enquiry should be treated as an FoI request and staff should follow procedures, which may require passing the request to a designated contact to assess the validity of the request and to decide how to respond. If the information falls into one of the categories in the information scheme and is already published, requesters should be informed of how and where to find the information. If the information is not part of the publication scheme, there should be procedures in place to decide whether to accept the request, search for the information and how to respond to the requester.

The response should be to provide the information requested, request any clarifications required to help the authority fulfil the request, or an explanation if the request has been refused. If the requester is not content with the response, they may request a review of the decision, so documenting the search for information or the reasons for refusing the request will provide a vital reference source for any similar requests in the future. The ICO provides a useful flowchart summarising the process of responding to FoI requests.[5]

Codes of practice

FoI law requires government to provide codes of good practice (Freedom of Information Act 2000, ss. 45 & 46; Freedom of Information (Scotland) Act 2002, ss. 60 & 61). The Information Commissioner's Office has issued FoI (Cabinet Office, 2018) and records management codes of practice (2016). It is not mandatory to adopt these codes. However, it makes sense to do so, as the ICO recognises authorities that have adopted the code of practice as having met their obligation to help members of the public exercise their rights (Information Commissioner's Office, 2018, 4).

The FoI code provides practical guidance on practice and provides links to more detailed information. As well as providing assistance to the public, the code covers fees, transferring requests to other authorities if the information is held by them, consultation with third parties about releasing

---

5. https://ico.org.uk/media/for-organisations/documents/1167/flowchart_of_request_handling_under_foia.pdf

information, confidentiality obligations and complaints procedures. LIK services may have contracts with suppliers or other parties that include confidentiality clauses, but FoI law may place limitations on those clauses. The records management code includes guidance on policy, training, storage, security and access and disposal schedules.

Top tips

Consider implementing an approach to requests for information as shown below:

Data protection subject access requests

Remember:

◆ they can be from any individual
◆ they can be to any organisation
◆ but they can only request personal data about themselves
◆ exemptions apply.

FoI requests

Remember:

◆ they can be from anyone
◆ they can be only to specific types of organisation
◆ they can be about anything
◆ exemptions apply (e.g. for anything with personal data).

Tools and templates

Introduction

Organisations drawing up procedures to implement information policies can make use of various sources of guidance, tools, and pro-formas. The main source of authoritative and detailed guidance on data protection and FoI is the Information Commissioner's Office (ICO). The Scottish Information Commissioner also provides FoI advice and toolkits for public authorities and other organisations subject to FoI in Scotland. The UK IPO provides some information and guidance on rights management, but little in the way of tools or templates to support this. Other sources of guidance on copyright and licensing include Jisc, which supports the higher and further education sectors in the UK in licensing and managing information resources. CopyrightUser.org provides advice on using copyright works for rights holders as well as copyright users, including libraries and archives. This chapter introduces sources of advice to help organisations comply with information laws and manage their own, and others' intellectual property appropriately. It also introduces toolkits and templates that organisations and LIK services can use in the development and implementation of their procedures.

Copyright and licensing agreements

Contractual arrangements are the main basis of intellectual property rights (IPR) management in organisations, including libraries and archives. As far as an organisation's own IPR are concerned, standard agreements can be drawn up to ensure the organisation owns rights in accordance with its policies. They can be effected through standard employment terms and other standardised contractual arrangements with service providers and independent consultants. The organisation's legal experts will normally draw up such standard agreements, but it is important to ensure that there is some flexibility to reflect the organisation's values and the different relationships it has with its stakeholders, so ensuring that the standardised agreements are fit for purpose and that each party gets what they need from the agreement.

LIK services are more concerned with the use of copyright works in their collections, including reprographic copying and scanning. There are various copyright exceptions for libraries (discussed elsewhere in this book and in standard texts), but much of this use will be governed by blanket licence agreements with collective licensing agencies, particularly the Copyright Licensing Agency (CLA) but also the Newspaper Licensing Agency (known as NLA media access) for newspapers, magazines and news websites, and other agencies providing sector-specific licences for non-text copyright works, including the Design and Artists Copyright Society (DACS), the Educational Recording Agency (ERA), PRS for Music, and Filmbankmedia. The CLA provides a tool for tracking the permissions contained in each type of licence.[1] The CLA now operates a Digital Content Store[2] for the higher education sector, which can be integrated with library management systems. This service involves a repository of digitised extracts from books and journals and a workflow management tool. The aim is to streamline the rights and permissions workflow and reduce the administrative workload for libraries.

The further and higher education sectors also benefit from Jisc's services. Jisc supports libraries in various ways, including negotiating deals with content providers and providing electronic resource management services, including licence management and entitlement tracking.[3] The Jisc model licence[4] provides consistency and has been developed over time to meet the needs of the sector, including ensuring ongoing access. Jisc has recently run a pilot of its Transnational Education licence[5] to simplify the licensing of resources for overseas students.

---

1. www.cla.co.uk/check-permissions/search-publications?query=
2. www.cla.co.uk/digital-content-store
3. www.jisc.ac.uk/jisc-collections
4. www.jisc-collections.ac.uk/Help-and-information/How-Model-Licences-work/Guide-to-Model-Licence
5. www.jisc.ac.uk/transnational-education-licensing

The aim of open licensing is to make it easier to access, copy, adapt, combine and share copyright works. This is achieved by attaching open licences to works specifying what can and cannot be done with them. Open licences, which are often CC licences, grant permission for access, sharing and reusing works with few or no restrictions. Research outputs, including research data, are increasingly openly licensed. This does not necessarily have an impact on library and information service budgets as yet, as it is still necessary to subscribe to scholarly journals to provide access to outputs that are not licensed in this way. LIK services staff in research and education institutions will need to be aware of open licensing, the licensing policies of publishers and the copyright status of educational resources if they are managing institutional repositories and support services for research outputs, research data or open educational resources. Libraries can use standard forms and agreements for the deposit of copyright works in institutional or subject-based repositories. This includes PhD theses, as well as self-archiving of preprints. Examples of thesis deposit forms are readily available online. They are submitted at the same time as the final bound version of the thesis. Using the form, the author confirms how the thesis can be accessed and used, including any embargo periods. For journal articles, the SHERPA/RoMEO service[6] allows librarians to search for publisher copyright and self-archiving policies. The database can be searched by publisher, journal name or ISSN.

Appendix 4, p. 175, provides some possible model clauses for an online access to databases agreement.

Copyright compliance and risk management

As discussed in Chapters 1 and 6, copyright compliance requires detailed knowledge of the copyright status of works in the organisation, permissions granted for use of works and monitoring this use. An organisation's tolerance of risk will inform its approach to compliance and to the management of its own IP. While librarians have the reputation of being risk-averse, progress in the development of library services and digital libraries cannot realistically be made by taking no risks at all. An example is the libraries involved in the Google Books library project. There is a history of rights holders (often slowly) accepting new uses of copyright

---

6. http://sherpa.ac.uk/romeo/index.php

works and licensing accordingly when these activities become normal practice that is expected by library and information service users.

Copyright compliance procedures should be informed by a risk management plan, which provides guidelines for how third-party content can be used. Risk assessment should consider what might happen if there is unauthorised use of copyright works and what steps could be taken to remove or reduce any risks identified. Various risk management calculators are available.[7] User (mis)behaviour may be the most likely risk for LIK services, but such unlawful behaviour on the part of users can be prevented or reduced by TPMs, acceptable use policies and copyright notices, as well as appropriate training and education programmes for users. The Libraries and Archives Copyright Alliance (LACA) provides helpful resources to support compliance, including an information poster for users that can be displayed in libraries[8] and model copyright declaration forms for library copying for users.[9]

Another source of risk in libraries is digitisation of works to make them more accessible. CopyrightUser.org provides general advice on how to calculate if a work is out of copyright, i.e., in the public domain[10] and on the use and reuse of copyright works for libraries.[11] Europeana provides a public domain calculator tool for different European countries.[12] There are tools to support diligent searches for rightsholders and identifying the copyright status of works. For example, the Writers Artists and their Copyright Holders (WATCH) database identifies rights holders and provides contact details.[13] The Firms Out of Business (FOB) database can be useful when searching for publishers or agencies that no longer exist. The European Intellectual Property Office maintains a database of orphan works.[14] However, this database is not comprehensive, as there are currently only around 6000 entries in it. Accessible Registries of Rights Information and Orphan Works (ARROW) is another European database created by a collaboration of libraries, publishers and collective

7. For example see www.cilip.org.uk/news/426274/A-useful-guide-to-copyright-tools-and-resources.htm
8. http://uklaca.org/304
9. http://uklaca.org/325
10. www.copyrightuser.org/create/public-domain/duration
11. www.copyrightuser.org/educate/intermediaries/libraries
12. http://archive.outofcopyright.eu
13. https://norman.hrc.utexas.edu/watch
14. https://euipo.europa.eu/ohimportal/en/web/observatory/orphan-works-db

management organisations.[15] The database provides information for anyone wishing to deal with orphan works. In the UK, the IPO maintains a register of orphan works, which contains information on applications for orphan works licences and the decisions made, that is, the licences granted and the applications that have been refused. There are currently (November 2019) around 900 entries in the database.

If a rights holder alleges copyright infringement, then notice and take-down procedures come into play. It is relatively simple to find examples of academic library take-down notices. This is probably because these libraries are more likely to hold alternative versions of published works, such as journal article preprints. For example, Leicester University Library has published its notice on its website along with its take-down policy.[16] The normal procedure when receiving a complaint that the library is making available copyright infringing materials is to take down the potentially infringing material whilst the complaint is investigated. It may be decided that what is being offered is not infringing, perhaps because it is appropriately licensed, the material is out of copyright, or the material is being made available under an appropriate exception to copyright. It may also be decided that the complaint is invalid, as the complainant has not established that it is the owner of the copyright or does not have the authority to act on behalf of the owner. In all such circumstances, it is appropriate to engage with the complainant.

Copyright, licensing and library management systems

Library management systems support the discovery, acquisition, accession and organisation of collections and control their use. Increasingly, access to institutional repositories is integrated into library management systems. Library management systems also integrate with supplier systems to streamline workflows. Licensing agreements for electronic resources will be implemented through the management system. Copyright and licensing information will also be added to records in institutional and subject repositories, so that users know what they may or may not do with content.

---

15. https://joinup.ec.europa.eu/collection/einclusion/document/accessible-registries-rights-information-and-orphan-works-arrow
16. https://www2.le.ac.uk/library/about/collectionpolicy/disclaimer-take-down-policy

Digital asset management systems

Digital asset management systems (DAMs) can organise, store and retrieve various types of assets, together with software for the management of rights and permissions. DAMs can range from simple linked spreadsheets to much more complicated databases with sophisticated functionality. There is a role for these systems in the management of digital resources and their associated rights and permissions, particularly because it is increasingly becoming harder to associate resources, such as images, with consent forms associated with the inclusion of any individuals as well as any permissions that relate to potential copyright in the resource itself. Although primarily associated with marketing departments of large organisations, they can also be used to manage the resources handled by LIK managers. An overview of commercially available DAM softwares is available.[17]

Privacy by design

Data protection law requires that organisations implement effective technological procedures to protect personal data and the rights of data subjects. The terms 'privacy by design', or 'privacy by design and by default' in GDPR terms, refers to the integration of data protection into all activities involving data processing from the design stage through to implementation. This includes setting up systems for responding to subject access requests and complaints about the organisation's data-processing activities.

The Information and Privacy Commissioner of Ontario (Cavoukian, 2011) developed the concept of the seven foundational principles of privacy by design:

◆ 'Proactive not Reactive; Preventative not Remedial
◆ Privacy as the Default Setting
◆ Privacy Embedded into Design
◆ Full Functionality – Positive-Sum, not Zero-Sum
◆ End-to-End Security – Full Lifecycle Protection
◆ Visibility and Transparency – Keep it Open
◆ Respect for User Privacy – Keep it User-Centric'.

---

17. www.softwareadvice.com/uk/cms/digital-asset-management-comparison

These principles should be implemented through business practices as well as IT systems and infrastructures. This, of course, includes LIK services. The ICO provides a checklist to help organisations understand what steps are required to take a privacy by design approach.[18]

- ◆ 'We consider data protection issues as part of the design and implementation of systems, services, products and business practices.
- ◆ We make data protection an essential component of the core functionality of our processing systems and services.
- ◆ We anticipate risks and privacy-invasive events before they occur, and take steps to prevent harm to individuals.
- ◆ We only process the personal data that we need for our purposes(s), and that we only use the data for those purposes.
- ◆ We ensure that personal data is automatically protected in any IT system, service, product, and/or business practice, so that individuals should not have to take any specific action to protect their privacy.
- ◆ We provide the identity and contact information of those responsible for data protection both within our organisation and to individuals.
- ◆ We adopt a 'plain language' policy for any public documents so that individuals easily understand what we are doing with their personal data.
- ◆ We provide individuals with tools so they can determine how we are using their personal data, and whether our policies are being properly enforced.
- ◆ We offer strong privacy defaults, user-friendly options and controls, and respect user preferences.
- ◆ We only use data processors that provide sufficient guarantees of their technical and organisational measures for data protection by design.
- ◆ When we use other systems, services or products in our processing activities, we make sure that we only use those whose designers and manufacturers take data protection issues into account.
- ◆ We use privacy-enhancing technologies (PETs) to assist us in complying with our data protection by design obligations.'

---

18. https://ico.org.uk/for-organisations/guide-to-data-protection/guide-to-the-general-data-protection-regulation-gdpr/accountability-and-governance/data-protection-by-design-and-default

Data protection compliance assessment

The ICO has provided a toolkit to help organisations assess their compliance with data protection law. The toolkit[19] is aimed at small to medium-sized enterprises. It includes checklists to help organisations acting as data controllers[20] and/or data processors.[21] The toolkit covers various processing activities: information security; direct marketing (which is covered by the Privacy and Electronic Communication Regulations as well as data protection law); records management; data sharing and access; and CCTV.

The controller checklist asks the extent to which the organisation has implemented key aspects of data protection. Possible responses are: not yet implemented or planned; partially implemented or planned; successfully implemented; or not applicable. When responses are submitted, specific and contextualised advice is offered, based upon the responses to each question. The order in which the questions are presented indicate the logical order in which organisations should tackle compliance, starting with the information audit to identify and record existence and nature of information assets and areas of risk, moving on to legal bases for processing, data subject rights, security, breaches and accountability issues. Links to the ICO's more detailed guidance documents are also presented in context. The data processor checklist includes similar questions but also some that are specific to the processor, such as use of processing contracts and sub-processors. The other checklists cover each specific area in more detail, so can help ensure that nothing important to compliance is overlooked. Where appropriate, they allow organisations to assess their policies, procedures and agreements. The ICO also offers audits and advisory visits to support organisations in assessment of their compliance with the law.[22] Audits can also cover FoI compliance. The purpose of advisory visits is to give advice on good practice and areas in which practice can be improved, focusing on records management, handling of subject access requests and security.

---

19. https://ico.org.uk/for-organisations/data-protection-self-assessment
20. https://ico.org.uk/for-organisations/data-protection-self-assessment/controllers-checklist
21. https://ico.org.uk/for-organisations/data-protection-self-assessment/processors-checklist
22. https://ico.org.uk/for-organisations/audits

Information audits and documentation

Organisations must document data-processing activities and auditing and mapping data flows is a necessary first step. The National Archives provides an overview of the possible ways of surveying information held by an organisation, including personal data.[23] Depending on the specific circumstances applying to an organisation, information specialists might survey the whole organisation at once, or by organisational unit, or each unit can survey its own data. The guidance points out the advantages and disadvantage of each approach. The ICO provides detailed guidance on documentation and templates for data controllers and data processors.[24] The ICO also provides guidance on identifying the lawful basis for processing, including an interactive tool.[25] Derbyshire County Council provides useful examples of how the GDPR requirements for documentation are met through registers: the information audit register; a contracts (personal data) register; data sharing agreements register; privacy impact assessments register; corporate and departmental risk registers.[26] Some organisations may prefer to make use of commercial audit services, such as those provided by some law firms, or specialist services such as Data Privacy Trust.[27]

The UK IPO provides IP Audit Services for small to medium-size organisations which support the commercialisation of IP assets.[28]

Privacy notices

Privacy notices are important in meeting the requirement for transparency, as they inform the public of what data will be collected, how it will be processed, who it will be shared with, their rights and how to contact the organisation to exercise their rights. Privacy notices are notorious for being overly long, written in inaccessible language and therefore not being read or understood by the public. The ICO provides a template privacy notice

---

23. www.nationalarchives.gov.uk/information-management/manage-information/policy-process/disposal/methods-finding-information/
24. https://ico.org.uk/for-organisations/guide-to-data-protection/guide-to-the-general-data-protection-regulation-gdpr/accountability-and-governance/documentation
25. https://ico.org.uk/for-organisations/gdpr-resources/lawful-basis-interactive-guidance-tool
26. www.derbyshire.gov.uk/working-for-us/data/gdpr/record-of-data-processing-activities/record-of-data-processing-activities.aspx
27. www.dataprivacytrust.com
28. www.ipo.gov.uk

that organisations can use as the basis for their own notices[29] – see Figure 9.1. This is a text document including several headings and providing some information on what should be included under each heading. There are various alternative approaches to how privacy notices can be presented, but the overriding consideration should be that the public is informed, so the language and the formatting are designed to facilitate this. The layered approach involves an overview document with all the basic information required to ensure transparency. The ICO template could be used as the first layer and could include links to more detailed information for each aspect of the privacy notice. The ICO uses a layered approach. A template privacy notice is provided in Appendix 5, p.183.

▌ICO Privacy notice   Share 🔗 Download options ⬇

Search this document 🔍   Darllenwch ein hysbysiad preifatrwydd yn Cymraeg.

1. General information   This privacy notice tells you what to expect us to do with your personal information when you make contact with us or use one of our services.

Controller's contact details

Data Protection Officer's   This notice is layered. So, if you wish, you can easily select the reason we process
contact details   your personal information and see what we do with it.

How do we get information?

Your data protection rights

Request a service adjustment

Sharing your information

Links to other websites

Your right to complain

Changes to this privacy notice

Children's information

Managing customer contact

How you can contact us   If your network blocks YouTube, you may not be able to view the above video. Please use another device.

Visitors to our website

Visitors to the office   Pressing play on the video above will set a third-party cookie. Please read our cookie policy for more information.

2. Reason for contacting us   Depending on your organisation's network policies, you may be unable to view the video on this page. In this case, please access the page on a non-network device.

Report a nuisance call or
message   We'll tell you:

Figure 9.1 *ICO layered privacy notice*

The ICO privacy notice contains headings so that the public can select sections they are interested in. Each section provides basic information and there are also links to further information. The introduction to the policy includes a video presentation, so the public has a choice in how they consume the information. Just-in-time notices – that is, highly specific and

---

29. https://ico.org.uk/media/for-organisations/documents/2259798/pn-template-microbusiness-201908.docx

contextualised notices – can be displayed to members of the public as they go through the process of providing personal data, for example when they provide contact details. These notices can say why the information is being collected and what will be done with it. This could be used, for example, when library users register to use services.

Icons have the potential to aid understanding, but care should be taken to ensure that any icons used can be easily understood by anyone. The CC licence iconography is an example of a simple and successful approach using a small number of icons whose meaning is clear across languages and cultures (Holtz, Nocun and Hansen, 2011). There's no standard iconography as yet in the privacy field. There have been attempts to develop such an iconography, but these have not generated wider interest or use. One example is the iconset developed by Matthias Mehldau (2007), see Figure 9.2.

Iconset for Data-Privacy Declarations v0.1

Let's simple declare what data is how used, stored, given away or deleted.

Figure 9.2 *Iconset for data-privacy declarations* (Mehldau, 2007)

The meaning of at least some of the icons in Mehldau's scheme may not be readily understandable, and a simplified approach with a smaller number of icons, such as the CC licence icons, seems to be more usable, so limited use of icons may work better in the privacy field. The PrimeLife project developed a small set of icons for general use accompanied by supplementary sets of icons for specific contexts, such as e-commerce or social media (Holtz, Nocun and Hansen, 2011). Whatever approach is adopted, it is good practice to test out draft notices with a representative sample of the public to ensure they are informative, readable and presented in accessible formats.

Privacy impact assessments

Privacy impact assessments play an important role in privacy by design, as their purpose is to ensure that organisations consider the privacy and data protection implications of a proposed activity before it is implemented. The ICO provides a screening checklist to help organisations identify when an impact assessment should be carried out[30] and a sample template for documenting the assessment.[31]

Reporting personal data breaches

The GDPR introduced some new responsibilities with regard to reporting data breaches. The ICO and the EDPB have provided detailed guidance on reporting breaches.[32, 33] This guidance should be reflected in the procedures organisations put in place to recognise and report breaches as required by the law. This includes guidance on contracts between data controllers and data processors and their respective liabilities[34] as well as responsibilities under privacy in electronic communications law[35] and electronic identification and trust services laws.[36]

Freedom of information publication schemes

All public authorities and other organisations that fall within the scope of

---

30. https://ico.org.uk/for-organisations/guide-to-data-protection/guide-to-the-general-data-protection-regulation-gdpr/accountability-and-governance/data-protection-impact-assessments

31. https://ico.org.uk/media/for-organisations/documents/2553993/dpia-template.docx

32. https://ico.org.uk/for-organisations/guide-to-data-protection/guide-to-the-general-data-protection-regulation-gdpr/personal-data-breaches

33. https://ec.europa.eu/newsroom/article29/item-detail.cfm?item_id=612052

34. https://ico.org.uk/media/about-the-ico/consultations/2014789/draft-gdpr-contracts-guidance- v1-for-consultation-september-2017.pdf

35. https://ico.org.uk/for-organisations/guide-to-pecr/communications-networks-and-services/security-breaches

36. https://ico.org.uk/for-organisations/guide-to-eidas

FoI laws in the UK must use a publication scheme approved by the ICO. The ICO has provided two versions of a model scheme: one for public bodies that are only covered by the legislation for some types of information, and the other for all other public bodies. Publication schemes should set out the classes of information to be published, the form in which the information will be made available and whether any charge will be made for the information. The publication scheme or associated information page should provide contact details for any queries or requests. The ICO provides guidance on charging for information.[37] Public authorities cannot levy charges that are not set out in the publication scheme. Any charges made for information published in accordance with the authority's publication scheme should be reasonable and for the following purposes:

> for communicating the information, such as photocopying and postage. We do not consider it reasonable to charge for providing information online; fees permitted by other legislation; and for information produced commercially, for example, a book, map or similar publication that you intend to sell and would not otherwise have produced.[38]

The public authority should make it clear how it calculates charges unless they are part of a statutory charging scheme. The ICO has no statutory duty to approve charges but does advise that maximum charges should be set and this should be done with the principle of encouraging public access to information in mind. Public authorities may be able to charge for reuse of a dataset over and above any charge for making the dataset available (Freedom of Information (Release of Datasets for Re-use) (Fees) Regulations 2013). However, if reuse of a dataset is authorised under the Open Government Licence,[39] then a reuse fee is not allowed.

Publication schemes should also clarify who owns the copyright in the information provided and what requesters can do with the information provided, in order to leave no doubt. For example, the British Library's

---

37. https://ico.org.uk/for-organisations/guide-to-freedom-of-information/charging-for-information-in-a-publication-scheme

38. https://ico.org.uk/for-organisations/guide-to-freedom-of-information/publication-scheme

39. www.nationalarchives.gov.uk/doc/open-government-licence/version/2

scheme authorises sharing and adapting information as long as the information is attributed to the British Library.[40]

The classes of information identified in the two versions of the model schedule[41] are:

Who we are and what we do
Organisational information, locations and contacts, constitutional and legal governance.

What we spend and how we spend it
Financial information relating to projected and actual income and expenditure, tendering, procurement and contracts.

What our priorities are and how we are doing
Strategy and performance information, plans, assessments, inspections and reviews.

How we make decisions
Policy proposals and decisions. Decision making processes, internal criteria and procedures, consultations.

Our policies and procedures
Current written protocols for delivering our functions and responsibilities.

Lists and registers
Information held in registers required by law and other lists and registers relating to the functions of the authority.

The services we offer
Advice and guidance, booklets and leaflets, transactions and media releases. A description of the services offered.

The model scheme for bodies only covered for certain information includes the same categories of information, but these bodies do not have to include information that is not easily accessible, for example if it has been placed in archival storage. Information in draft form is also excluded. The ICO has provided templates for different types of public authorities, including small authorities, such as medical practices, schools and parish councils.[42]

---

40. www.bl.uk/about-us/freedom-of-information
41. https://ico.org.uk/for-organisations/guide-to-freedom-of-information/publication-scheme
42. https://ico.org.uk/for-organisations/guide-to-freedom-of-information/publication-scheme/definition-documents

The UK's national libraries have their own publication schemes.[43–45] Other LIK services that are under the control of a body subject to FoI (including libraries and information services of national and local government departments, schools, colleges and universities) will be covered by their parent body's scheme. The BBC is one of the public bodies that is only partially covered by FoI legislation. The BBC's scheme only includes information relating to its constitution and how it is run. It does not cover information relating to programming activities. The formatting of the BBC's scheme is worth noting for its visually appealing presentation (see Figure 9.3).

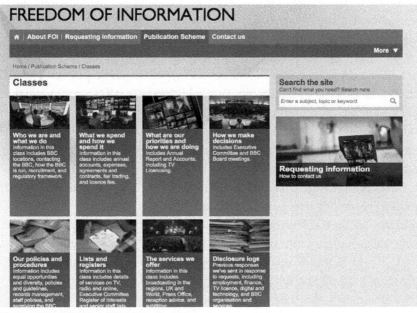

Figure 9.3 *BBC FoI publication scheme*

The House of Commons scheme presents the categories of information on its web pages, but the details are provided in a downloadable Excel file.[46] Public authorities should consider how best to present their schemes

43. The British Library's publication scheme www.bl.uk/about-us/freedom-of-information/1-who-we-are-and-what-we-do
44. The National Library of Wales' publication scheme www.library.wales/about-nlw/governance/freedom-of-information-act/publication-scheme
45. The National Library of Scotland's publication scheme www.nls.uk/about-us/freedom-of-information
46. www.parliament.uk/site-information/foi/accessing-information

and provide access to their information to ensure it is as straightforward as possible for the public to find information.

Dealing with freedom of information requests

The law requires that public authorities normally must respond to FoI requests within 20 working days. Good information management procedures and actions will make it easier to comply with this obligation. There should also be procedures in place to ensure that decisions on whether to supply the information, whether a charge should be made, or whether an exemption applies are taken in a timely fashion. The ICO's guidance documents on responding to requests are helpful in that they take a layered approach through links to more detailed advice on increasingly specific questions authorities may have. The ICO also provides a useful overview flowchart for responding to requests.[47] The ICO chart is complemented by more detailed information.[48] Given the purpose of freedom of information, public bodies should be cautious, and must give careful consideration before refusing a request. Again, the ICO provides an overview and more detailed guidance on the various reasons for refusal.[49] The ICO provides advice on how to safely withhold information,[50] for example personal data. The National Archives provides a redaction toolkit.[51] Some of this guidance is only relevant to records and archival material to be transferred to The National Archives. However, it does provide useful guidance on what redaction is and how to identify material that should be redacted. If the decision is to refuse a request, the ICO provides guidance on what to include in a refusal notice.[52] Requesters have the right to appeal if they are unhappy with a decision.

---

47. https://ico.org.uk/media/for-organisations/documents/1167/flowchart_of_request_handling_under_foia.pdf
48. https://ico.org.uk/for-organisations/guide-to-freedom-of-information/receiving-a-request
49. https://ico.org.uk/for-organisations/guide-to-freedom-of-information/refusing-a-request
50. https://ico.org.uk/media/for-organisations/documents/how-to-disclose-information-safely-removing-personal-data-from-information-requests-and-datasets/2013958/how-to-disclose-information-safely.pdf
51. www.nationalarchives.gov.uk/documents/information-management/redaction_toolkit.pdf
52. https://ico.org.uk/media/for-organisations/documents/1211/refusing_a_request_writing_a_refusal_notice_foi.pdf

Top tips

1   Readers of this book based in the UK should refer to guidance, templates and other tools provided by the UK IPO and the ICO and the template privacy notice in Appendix 5 to save time and effort and to help ensure compliance with the law and provision of efficient and effective services based on personal data and public information. Other readers should also find these resources useful.

2   Look and learn from the practices of other organisations rather than reinventing wheels.

10 Awareness and engagement

Introduction

This chapter explores the role of information law awareness and engagement from both an operational and strategic perspective. It will be of importance and interest to LIK workers, who may:

◆ require ongoing training themselves in information law compliance issues, such as copyright, data protection and freedom of information
◆ have responsibility for raising awareness and ensuring engagement amongst their colleagues, students and possibly volunteers
◆ need to make the business case to senior management for training and development as a long-term commitment on behalf of their organisation
◆ need to develop a long-term strategy, supported by a business case, for maintaining high levels of awareness and engagement beyond training
◆ need to find a budget to support ongoing training and awareness activities.

High levels of staff awareness and engagement with information law issues are essential to organisational compliance with the law, whilst the proceeding chapters have also discussed the relationship between legal compliance and proportionality regarding risk. This means that inefficiencies and/or mistakes in the management of information law issues and the lack of awareness and staff confidence in managing rights, permissions and consents can increase risk, hamper opportunities and duplicate efforts, increasing overall costs and reducing the impact of information law policies and their implementation, as well as reducing access to information. Thus, raising awareness and engagement with information law issues is both an operational and a strategic imperative. It's an operational issue because awareness of information law compliance and its application to a specific organisation enables staff to do their jobs better. It's also a strategic issue, because organisations with limited resources for training, awareness raising and engagement need to ensure that they plan how they can optimise staff understanding of the issues, who to target and also achieve the long-term embedding of such knowledge into the corporate memory. Moreover, legal compliance issues often require the maintenance of high levels of staff awareness so that long-term investment is made in retaining good levels of awareness amongst current staff, whilst also training up new starters.

Benefits of engaging with information law issues

The fear of dealing with legal compliance issues by staff because of low levels of awareness about the issues has meant that often these issues fail to be embedded within organisational policies, procedures or basic staff or student competencies. Instead, some organisations have overly relied upon legal professionals who are brought in to put right things that would and should have never gone wrong in the first place. Furthermore, a lack of awareness and engagement can result in the following:

◆ the denial of key skills development for staff, such as negotiation skills
◆ the risk of cavalier approaches or overly risk-averse positions
◆ organisations failing to consider the role of risk management and consequently failing to consider how risks might be mitigated
◆ a reduction in the ability of organisations to deal as efficiently as they could with content and data creation, curation, access, storage and use
◆ duplication of costs when organisations may be paying more than once for access to the same resources.

For these reasons, awareness and engagement sit at the very basis of compliance. This is because boosting staff confidence in information law issues, such as copyright, data protection and freedom of information, can help them feel confident to incorporate information law within organisational culture, and at the same time help ensure that a more risk-aware culture is embraced. As a result, it is then possible to build a privacy and rights by design culture, because everyone can take responsibility for incorporating legal compliance into project management considerations, resource and budget calculations and issues associated with staff time and expertise. For example, staff who are confident and aware of information law issues can ensure that high-risk activities, such as the procurement of services from external contractors, have a better chance of being supported by robust intellectual property right clauses which are favourable to the LIK services which have contracted them, whilst also ensuring that any data-processing activities are supported by the necessary data privacy clauses.

Training

LIK workers will often find that the responsibility for engagement and awareness with information law compliance issues falls to them. It is important to recognise that whilst training is only one aspect of raising awareness, training can take various forms, which include:

◆ face-to-face training
 — organisational scheduled onsite training and briefing sessions run for departments and/or across the organisation
 — ad hoc training supporting the induction of new starters
 — attendance at externally provided training courses
 — departmental updates
 — training by Skype and/or video conferencing
◆ e-learning
 — off-the-shelf and/or bespoke organisational tutorials. There are plenty available on data protection and information security for example, which use a combination of text, film and audio and self-assessment testing.
 — registration on externally provided tutorials[1]
◆ registration on a short course with professional qualifications, such as that provided by the Institute of Art and Law[2] and King's College

---

1. For example www.futurelearn.com/courses/film-copyright

Post Graduate Qualification in UK, EU and US Copyright Law,[3] as well as certification through organisations like CC.[4]

♦ webinar attendance. CILIP[5] regularly provides a number of information law compliance webinars for members and non-members
♦ conferences, one-day events and seminars.

Choosing the appropriate way to provide training for staff is an important decision and may be a combination of the above according to budget, user needs, prior knowledge and organisational priorities. Information law training is hard fought over and when you get your budget, it is important that your training is effective, as it may only come round once a year, or less frequently. Here are some top tips for both planning and delivering information law training for colleagues, which will hopefully encourage impactful changes and support your broader information law compliance objectives.

Planning your session

♦ Identify learning objectives before you start planning your session.
♦ Consider your audience and their specific needs. What about data protection, copyright or FoI is most important to your audience? Why are you having the training? Who is involved? What are the desired outcomes?
♦ Create learning that is memorable.
♦ Build into your training some of the awareness-raising ideas below.
♦ Training should be inclusive and encourage engagement but not everyone wants to be the centre of attention. Use a mix of group work and self-appointed group leaders to cater for all types of personalities in the room.
♦ Always use case studies, stories and empathy. Use news stories and real-world examples to explain points, particularly if the points are difficult to understand. Reading sections of the legislation is not helpful and creates fear.
♦ Will resources help the training? Perhaps you are training colleagues

---

2. https://ial.uk.com
3. www.kcl.ac.uk/law/research/centres/european/programmes/copyright
4. https://certificates.creativecommons.org
5. www.cilip.org.uk

and want them to learn how to use new resources, for example a data breach procedure, correctly. In these cases, make the learning scenario-based.

◆ If you are training colleagues, they may be there out of an organisational requirement rather than choice. You will need to sell the importance of the subject! Why is it important to the business? Why is it important to their role? What will they learn as part of the training? All of these questions need to be covered.

◆ Remember that information law is a big topic and so training can only achieve so much, particularly in a day and more so if you have less time. Sometimes helping participants remember key principles (with creative learning techniques), and encouraging them to think about the right questions to ask, is as positive as you might get.

Delivering your session

◆ There is a tendency for people to accede to scare-mongering with information law and to overcomplicate the subject. Make the subject simple; only give the necessary information and give lots of reassurance.

◆ Don't forget the post-lunch lull and the need to reinvigorate your audience's attention.

◆ There is nothing like learning with Post-It notes and flipchart paper rather than reading from a bulleted PowerPoint list. If you do use PowerPoint, try to use images as much as possible and direct your training to your audience instead of talking to a wall!

◆ Make a connection: begin the session by giving each member of staff a name tag and/or giving each person the opportunity to introduce themselves and say what they hope to gain by attending the session. This increases the involvement of each delegate as well as giving you extra insight into the personalities and knowledge level in the room.

Case study 10.1: Library provision of institutional copyright training

A library based in a university with several hundred staff requires all staff to be aware of copyright issues in order to support staff and users in gaining lawful access to electronic resources and journal articles. Twice a year, the library provides a full-day basic introduction to the topic provided by one expert, followed by two subsequent full-day sessions examining the practical implementation of copyright, provided by another expert. Both sessions enable questions raised by staff to be addressed by the expert, are supported by comprehensive resources and include practical exercises.

Role of games

Over the last few years, much has been written about the use of games to engage and support learning, and information law issues such as copyright and data protection have not been immune from 'gamification' to encourage learning. These games include quiz myth and reality cards produced by Copyright User[6] and board games, such as those based on bingo, snakes and ladders and other card games.[7] But playing games is not new in such training. Copyright training has often incorporated quizzes, and some of the first sector-wide copyright training provided by Collections Trust[8] over two decades ago for museum staff introduced the notion of game playing to raise awareness and engagement. Nonetheless, playing games is an important approach, and using games offers an engaging way to involve different audiences and support inclusive learning.

An enjoyable, innovative and useful tool for introducing copyright to those less familiar with it is 'Copyright: the card game'. Intended for use in small groups, with a tutor who is familiar with copyright, it introduces the basic ideas of what works are subject to copyright, how long copyright in them lasts, what the major exceptions to copyright are, and sources of licences. There are versions of the game for UK, US, and Canadian law. Details can be found at https://copyrightliteracy.org/resources/copyright-the-card-game/. The cards themselves and associated Powerpoint presentation are available under a Creative Commons licence.

Train the trainer

Train the trainer sessions are ideal opportunities to increase the skills of staff who understand copyright well and intend to act as copyright

---

6. www.copyrightuser.org
7. See, for example, www.cilip.org.uk/news/426429/The-Copyright-Card-Game.htm
8. www.collectionstrust.org.uk

champions for their team and/or department. These normally enable participants to try different training techniques and explore new innovative techniques that work for them, as well as enable participants to share ideas with each other. Train the trainer sessions can also help develop transferable train-the-trainer skills sets applicable to other topics.

Training needs analysis

To assess the type of need for training, a brief training needs analysis is extremely useful in informing the development of a learning and development strategy to support information law compliance. It can target training needs and help ensure that limited training resources are used wisely. Such an analysis, via online surveys, as well as certain face-to-face discussions with targeted staff, will inform what an organisation might cover in generic corporate information law compliance training, as well as establishing the focus for more specific face-to-face training. It can establish who needs what, why and how, as well as start to address the key topics. It can also provide some useful user intelligence for ideas that might be welcome to provide ongoing awareness activities subsequent to the training.

A training needs analysis template is provided below. It can be fine tuned to cover copyright, data protection, FoI, etc.

1 What would you consider to be your general level of awareness and understanding of information law?
   a. Very high
   b. High
   c. Average
   d. Low
   e. Very low
   f. Don't know
   g. ADD A COMMENT
2 When drawing up contracts for suppliers and associates, do you examine carefully the IP, data protection and or/FoI clauses?
   a. Yes
   b. No
   c. Sometimes
   d. Other, e.g. not part of my current duties, please specify
3 What types of generic issues relating to information law do you want to learn through training? (tick as many that apply)

    a.   Latest legislative developments and relevant court decisions

    b.   International issues

    c.   Protecting rights

    d.   Dealing with data breaches and infringements

    e.   SARs and FoI requests

    f.   General rights management issues

    g.   Legal compliance and the role of risk management

    h.   Permissions and consent

    i.   Information law and social media

    j.   General introduction to information law compliance

    k.   Other, please indicate

4   Where do you currently go to find out more about information law issues that might arise?

    a.   Internet

    b.   UK IPO and/or the ICO or their websites

    c.   Legal texts

    d.   Talk to an expert in our organisation

    e.   Ask a librarian and/or information professional

    f.   Training

    g.   Obtain formal legal advice

    h.   Other, please indicate

5   What, in your opinion is your general approach to dealing with risks associated with information law compliance?

    a.   I am comfortable taking risks within the context of a risk managed approach

    b.   I hesitate to take risks

    c.   I am completely risk-averse

    d.   Other, please indicate

6   If you have already received information law-related training, what have you received?

    a.   N/A

    b.   From an external consultant

    c.   From the in-house legal team and/or in-house library/information staff

    d.   Webinars

    e.   Attended a short course

    f.   Attended a conference, one-day event and/or a seminar

    g.   Completed a law degree

h. As part of a non-law degree, e.g., an information studies degree
i. Mentoring
j. Other, please indicate

7 If you have already received information law-related training, when did you last receive it?
a. Within the last 6 months
b. Within the last 6–12 months
c. Over a year ago
d. More than 2 years ago
e. More than 4 years ago
f. Other, please indicate

8 How often do you think updates to training would be useful for you in your role?
a. At least every 6 months
b. Every 6–12 months
c. Every year
d. Every 2 years
e. Other, please indicate

9 What do you think would be the most effective way/s of using online training to raise awareness and understanding amongst staff?
a. Case studies
b. Web-based training
c. Structured progression requiring levels of understanding before moving to next section
d. Generic questions and answers
e. Signposts to further resources
f. Talking heads and incorporation of multimedia
g. Ability to ask copyright questions
h. Evaluated responses
i. Face-to-face training
j. Other, please indicate

10 If you are provided with specific face-to-face training, how long do you think the training should be?
a. 2 hours
b. ½ day
c. 1 day
d. Other, please indicate

11 Can you give examples of online training (not necessarily related to information law) that you have found particularly accessible and useful?
[FREE TEXT]

12 How might awareness of information law issues be maintained AFTER initial training?
   a. Regular updates
   b. Development of specific processes
   c. Development of specific tools
   d. Top-up training sessions
   e. Information law champions for each department/team/country
   f. Information law help desk
   g. Other, please indicate

13 Do you have any further comments that you would like to make regarding the provision of information law training?
[FREE TEXT]

Developing a long-lasting and integrated approach to information law awareness and engagement

Retaining a high level of information law awareness as well as staff engagement, however, is unlikely to be maintained just through training. The need to support staff is wider than this, and will require ongoing organisational commitment. Ways in which awareness and engagement can be maintained include:

♦ a specialist, such as named Copyright Officer and a named Data Protection/FoI Officer (which is a requirement for most organisations under the GDPR; it is quite possible that the same person could fill both roles)
♦ updated material on the staff intranet about legal compliance requirements
♦ staff attendance at external events as part of their professional development, feeding back to the organisation what they have learnt
♦ encouragement of staff to sit on professional committees on behalf of the organisation as subject specialist experts, such as the Libraries and Archives Copyright Alliance (LACA)[9]

---

9. http://uklaca.org

◆ copyright awareness days and/or months to heighten awareness
◆ high-visibility poster campaigns, such as those relating to the confidential shredding of paper records in accordance with data protection requirements and/or posters regarding copying limits
◆ the establishment of an Information Governance Board where information law issues can be raised, which is discussed in Chapter 4
◆ Departmental updates and short staff briefings on a regular basis and/or as specific issues arise, such as information security and data protection issues, etc.

Case study 10.2: Copyright training and awareness in a large global organisation

A large global organisation was concerned that staff based in offices across the world lacked basic copyright awareness, which exposed the organisation to reputational and financial risks. As a result, they employed a Copyright Officer who used a combination of webinars, staff surveys and tailor-made animations about key topics, such as 'copyright fundamentals', 'finding free images to use for free' and 'protecting rights', to raise staff awareness about copyright. These were then incorporated into a Copyright Awareness Month. Training needs analysis surveys carried out afterwards demonstrated the positive and far-reaching impact of this approach. High levels of awareness were maintained by regular departmental staff surgery sessions, training upon induction, and a copyright knowledge loop whereby questions asked during the copyright surgery sessions were integrated into a FAQs which were made available on the staff intranet.

Top tips

Ten ways to raise and maintain awareness about information law compliance:[10]

1   Create case studies and FAQs to demonstrate positive and negative outcomes.

---

10. Based upon blog posts written by Debbie McDonnell and Carol Tullo and available at www.naomikorn.com/news.

2   Try to write a short piece about a specific theme or issue, which you can add to your organisational newsletter or blog.
3   Identify staff champions who can galvanise their teams and act as a lightning rod for reporting back good and bad practices.
4   Catchphrases, acrostics, crosswords, and other word games: **Getting Data Protection Ready** or **Right** still works. Some have used hidden words in text to emphasise key terms like controller, breach, SAR. **Copy Right** also works well, as does **Copy Wrong**!
5   Quizzes linked to a hook or anniversary.
6   Using numbers: the GDPR countdown clock was a popular device leading up to 2018 but think about 72 hours, 20 days or the fine levels catching attention. Use any trigger that has meaning for your team – perhaps a major launch, event or exhibition.
7   Posters, use of shared information screens using memorable images, scenarios and facts.
8   Official notices, such as those based on freely downloadable posters provided by LACA.
9   Myth sheets and quizzes, which can be circulated to staff to update their knowledge.
10 Top tips and checklists downloadable from the staff intranet.

11 Some speculations about the future

Staff in LIK services are facing a challenging time. Technology is advancing apace, with exciting, yet potentially dangerous developments in artificial intelligence, and with new technologies for recording and processing personal data (such as face-recognition technologies, and the use of social media and home assistance devices such as Alexa) becoming commonplace. In the field of copyright, there have been developments both in technologies to make it easier to copy and disseminate materials to multiple audiences all over the world, and in TPM software to try to prevent easy infringement being applied. We now live in a world where everyone can be a content creator, often using multiple media, as well as a content disseminator, publisher and a content user. Sometimes we can be all of them, collectively with others. Social media platforms make it easier to share content and often blur these roles. Over the decades, the resulting role of the LIK professional has changed beyond recognition, with arguably an increased role as being an advisor on the legality of things as well as a completely changed intermediary role between the patron and the information they wish to access. But they are not the only one in that position. Increasingly sophisticated search engines, such as Google, as well as TDM and other computational analysis technologies, can quickly provide access to information, whilst the internet is becoming overwhelmed with fake news and other misleading and sometimes illegal content.

Information law is also standing rather like a piggy in the middle, again between content owners and content users. On the one hand, the law tries to encourage novel creations, freedom of expression and creativity. On the other hand, it tries to prevent abuse of the new technologies by means, for example, of data protection legislation and strong rights for content creators. However, the law faces particular challenges. The first is the tension between creators and users (in the case of copyright), or between privacy and exploitation of personal data (in the case of data protection). There is also the tension between the wish for accountable and open government so citizens are fully informed about, and can comment on, the actions of all levels of government (through freedom of information), and the wish by government agencies to maintain confidentiality for commercial or national security (or perhaps more sinister) reasons. The second challenge is the fact that, by their very nature, laws do not change rapidly at a national scale and move even more slowly at an international scale, and so they are unable to both respond and/or flex fast enough to new technological developments or changes to user habits and priorities. This creates an enormous tension between what is technologically possible and seen as desirable or normal and what is legally allowed – resulting in legal uncertainty, flouting of the current law, and large-scale commoditisation of both personal data and content. To a degree, GDPR and other UK and EU legislation, such as the EU Copyright Directive passed by the EU Parliament in 2019, has tried to address this, but definitely not entirely successfully, and there is still much work to be done to redress the current imbalance.

Finally, in the scholarly communications field, the tensions between those who favour Open Access and CC and those often highly profitable commercial publishers who dominate the marketplace show no sign of abating. This tension is typified in the requirement, often imposed by dominant scholarly publishers, that authors assign copyright to the publisher or are obliged to offer exclusive licences to the publisher, which similarly restrict the authors, their host institutions, users and funding bodies, rather than simply giving the publisher a less restrictive licence to reproduce. Combine all this with issues such as Brexit (for those in the UK), and the climate crisis (for everyone – see below), and we are truly facing a perfect storm of issues that information law, and the professionals that regularly interact with it, are currently facing.

There has been relatively little written about whether copyright itself, or the length of copyright terms are justified, but some interesting pieces have included Fine (2017), a short book by Martin (1998) and another by Stephan Kinsella (2015). Kinsella, who is a patent attorney, is arguably a gamekeeper turned poacher. In contrast, Boren (2016) praises the most extreme pro-IP activist of recent years, Joseph Galambos, who believed intellectual property should last indefinitely. As a curious aside, Boren's book is available under a CC licence. John Willinsky (2018) has also written on this topic; in his book, he asks what it is about learning that helped to create the idea of copyright, a concept with a completely different legal and economic standing to other sorts of property.

A new book (Brown, 2019) on climate change and IP explores the lack of overlap between intellectual property law and climate change law. It argues that intellectual property confers private rights on the results of innovation and creativity, while climate change law and policy is more in the public sphere, and there is a conflict between private IP powers and public goals as access to information required by the public and by decision makers is unavailable or unaffordable. The book proposes new processes for policy and law-making in order to assist. The mere fact that such a book has appeared is symptomatic of the unexpected ways in which copyright law interacts with global issues. A familiar complaint amongst Open Access activists is the fact that so much of the key literature of global warming is too expensive for decision makers in developing countries to read.

So where does this leave the information professional? All three authors of this book have been involved, to a greater or lesser extent, in activism in regard to information law. We have belonged to committees or associations that advise or lobby government, have been involved in research into, and written reports on, many aspects of current information law, sometimes highlighting problematic issues. But efforts, such as to reduce the wide range of exemptions offered to data and information owners in current data protection and FoI laws, or to reduce the power of copyright owners when they impose unreasonable contractual terms on authors and clients, or use their financial muscle to lobby governments, are often frustrated. We would certainly argue for exceptions to copyright to be changed into *rights* for information users, rather than tokens given with reluctance by copyright owners (Chapdelaine, 2017). The London Manifesto (Eblida, 2015) is an example of how European-based library and information associations have lobbied in the past for steps in this direction. More radically, we would also question the idea of the same duration of copyright for all works, and suggest that with the ubiquity of content creation, often made for the purposes of content sharing through social media platforms, not all content has the same commercial value or needs to have the same lifetimes, and therefore some kind of 'use it or lose it' principle should be built into the Berne Convention. We would further ague that exemptions to data protection and FoI laws should be reviewed, and that the funds and powers available to the ICO should be increased. Information law needs to be made more nimble, able to be amended faster than at present, and, if at all possible, the procedures and the balance of membership of international bodies such as the World Intellectual Property Organization[1] should be improved.

Legal compliance is an ongoing and continuous journey for all who work in LIK services. What we hope for most of all is that this book will not only assist readers in their travels on that journey by following our advice on how to deal with the current and future challenges that information law poses, but also to help lobby to make information law more relevant and helpful in the future.

---

1. https://en.wikipedia.org/wiki/World_Intellectual_Property_Organization

Appendix 1
Carrying out an information asset audit[1]

Organisations hold 'information assets'. An information or data asset is a body of information, defined and managed as a single unit so it can be understood, shared, protected and exploited effectively. Information assets have recognisable and manageable value, risk, content and lifecycles. The first step in GDPR compliance is an information asset audit. This will also help you map the data flows in your organisation and work out what data you are holding and how it supports your business.

An organisation needs to know:

1   which information assets it holds – this can be held in an Information Asset Register
2   which information assets contain personal data and sensitive personal data
3   detailed information about the basis of processing personal data within individual information assets.

Your data asset	Responses
What is the name and/or description of the information asset/s?	
Why are you processing the personal data in the asset?	
Who is the asset owner in your organisation (i.e. the member of staff responsible for collecting the information and/or in charge of the project and/or initiative involving personal data)?	

---

1. Based on a template created by Naomi Korn Associates.

Your data asset	Responses
Are you the data controller/processor or joint controller/processor?	
Whose personal data are you processing?	
Are you processing sensitive personal data?	
What are your lawful bases for processing?	
What permissions do you have for the processing of the data? Are these set out in a Privacy Notice associated with the collection of the data?	
Have you carried out a data privacy impact assessment (DPIA) for this data?	
Where is the personal data stored?	
Who has access to the information asset?	
How is the information asset kept safe? (IT security measures, but also including other physical, electronic and managerial procedures to safeguard and secure the information)	
How long do you keep the personal data in the asset? Is it up to date? Do you have an agreed retention period? Is this documented?	
What are the risks to the business from the asset for example from its loss, corruption or inappropriate access? What happens if something goes wrong and there is a data breach? Is there a documented process?	
Do you share the data with anyone? If so, what is your justification for this?	
Do your contracts reflect any arrangements you have made for sharing and storing the data?	
Is any of the data collected from third parties? Do you have the necessary consents from them to process their data?	

Appendix 2
Sample IP policy[1]

Definitions

Commercial Use Reproducing a work in any manner that is primarily intended for or directed toward commercial advantage or monetary compensation.

Crown Copyright Works deposited with the organisation that have been produced for or on behalf of the Crown.

Infringement Any unauthorised use of material, which is protected by copyright and/or any other related right, for which permission to use, has not been obtained. Infringements can occur in print and/or digital form.

Intellectual Property Rights (IPR/IP) All patents, Trade Marks, trade names and domain names, service marks, rights to inventions, copyright and related rights, rights in get-up, rights in goodwill, unfair competition rights, rights in designs (whether held in physical or electronic format or otherwise howsoever), database rights, rights in confidential information (including know-how and trade secrets) and any other intellectual property rights, in each case whether registered or unregistered and including all applications (and rights to apply) for, and renewal or extensions of, such rights and similar or equivalent rights or forms of protection in any part of the world.

Non-commercial Use Reproducing a work in any manner that is not primarily intended for or directed toward commercial advantage or monetary compensation.

Orphan Works Works that are in copyright, but where the owners of any third-party rights are either unknown or cannot be traced.

---

1. Based on a template created by Naomi Korn Associates.

Third-Party Rights Intellectual property rights, not owned by the organisation.

Works Items, objects and/or collections and/or content, both accessioned and support collections. It also applies to any assets created by the organisation's staff and/or anyone else working for, or on behalf of the organisation and/or involving the organisation.

1. Introduction

1.1 The organisation owns, creates, commissions, loans, acquires, has deposited and uses a wide range of Works. Intellectual Property Rights (IPR) protects many of these. This document sets out the organisation's policy regarding the use, access to and management of these IPR. It includes IPR owned by the organisation, as well as any IPR vesting in the organisation's Works for which a third party might own the IPR.

1.2 This Policy outlines a framework under which the organisation, its staff and those working for or on behalf of the organisation should operate to ensure legal compliance, reduce the organisation's exposure to risks and work in accordance with robust ethical and reputational imperatives. Moreover, adherence to this Policy supports the achievement of the organisation's strategic objectives.

2. Scope

2.1 This Policy applies to all types of relevant IPR

2.2 The organisation is subject to the provisions of the Copyright Designs and Patents Act 1988, as amended and revised, and other relevant legislation, regulations and internal policies.

3. Purpose

3.1 The purpose of this Policy is:

◆ to comply with the relevant legislation and reduce risks of infringement

◆ to ensure that staff and others working with the organisation understand their roles and responsibilities regarding IPR

- to increase awareness of the value of the organisation's IPR and to protect it wherever possible
- to facilitate the appropriate use of the organisation and Third-party Rights
- to ensure the optimum reuse of and access to Works which have been acquired, donated and/or deposited
- to ensure that the IPR are properly documented according to professional standards
- to acknowledge the importance of rights management across all of the organisation's activities.

4. Principles

4.1 The key principles governing the use of this Policy are:

- The organisation is committed to protect its IPR and Third Party Rights wherever possible.
- The organisation shall acquire IPR in its Works and, where this is not possible, a licence to enable the organisation to reproduce and use the Works for all its purposes.
- The organisation shall manage IPR within its internal policies and legislative commitments.
- The organisation shall explore opportunities where possible to exploit its IPR, both commercially and in helping to raise brand awareness.

5. Responsibilities

5.1 The CEO/Director is responsible for ensuring that the organisation has a robust IPR Policy, and that its staff and those working with or for the organisation are compliant with it. The CEO/Director has responsibility for delegating responsibility for the implementation of this Policy to Heads of Departments where appropriate.

5.2 Heads of Department are responsible for overseeing compliance across the organisation.

5.3 The IP Officer is responsible for assessing IPR-related risks and overseeing potential infringements of the organisation's IPR. They are also responsible for day-to-day advice and support to staff on copyright and related issues.

5.4 Line Managers are responsible for ensuring that their staff and those working with or for the organisation shall comply with this Policy and associated procedures.

5.5 Compliance with this Policy is a requirement for all employees, temporary and agency staff, contractors, volunteers, students, interns, placements and where appropriate, others working with and for the organisation.

6. Policy
6.1 Protecting IPR

6.1.1 IPR is a valuable asset for the organisation and other rights holders. The organisation is committed to protect its IPR and Third-party Rights wherever possible and ensure that appropriate procedures are in place to safeguard the organisation's IPR and support the principles outlined within this Policy.

6.1.2 Use of approved credit lines is an important requirement of the use of Works by the organisation and others.

6.1.3 The organisation should implement where appropriate other means to protect both the organisation's IPR and Third-party Rights, including copyright notices, trade mark registrations, re-use licences, image metadata and image size restrictions. This includes the mandatory maintenance of a Notice and Take-Down Policy.

6.2 Use of Works and other content by the organisation

6.2.1 The organisation is committed to respecting IPR. Unless usage can be justified under the UK's exceptions to copyright, the organisation makes every effort to trace any owners of Third-party Rights and obtain the necessary permissions so that the organisation can fully use and promote, safeguard and provide access to its Works.

6.2.2 Wherever possible, the organisation shall ensure that Third-party Rights are cleared either during or immediately subsequent to the acquisition and/or donation and/or depositing/lending of Works, using the appropriate documentation and in accordance with the relevant internal policies.

6.2.3 The organisation shall maintain a policy regarding the use of

Works on social media channels. Any use of these Works shall be in accordance with this Policy.

6.2.4 The organisation shall reproduce Orphan Works subject to the necessary reasonable searches, review of exceptions and licences as well as methods to mitigate risk.

6.3 Others using Works owned by the organisation

6.3.1 The organisation is committed, where possible, to providing access to copies of its Works in compliance with its statutory, regulatory and corporate objectives.

6.3.2 Commercial requests from third parties to use copies of Works should be directed to the Picture Library.

6.3.3 The organisation shall maintain a policy on public filming and photography in accordance with the principles outlined within this Policy, its data protection obligations and other legal and statutory obligations.

6.4 Ownership of IPR

6.4.1 The organisation shall strive to own the IPR in any Works produced for or, in partnership or on behalf of the organisation. Where this is not possible, the organisation shall ensure wherever possible that it reserves the right to reuse the Works for its own purposes, that its ability to commercially exploit the Works is not unduly restricted and where appropriate grant sub-licences along these same terms.

6.4.2 The IPR in anything produced by the organisation staff in the course of their duties are the property of the organisation. The IPR in anything produced by the organisation's staff in their own time and without any connection or reference to their employment at the organisation are their property.

6.4.3 Commissioned parties, freelancers and other contracted parties working for or on behalf of the organisation shall assign their IPR to the organisation using the appropriate agreements. Where this is not possible, they shall grant a licence to the organisation to enable reuse of their IPR for all the organisation's purposes. The organisation shall ensure that it has appropriate written agreements in place to negotiate the right to apply for and register worldwide any patent for an invention, Trade Mark and designs. In cases where this is not possible the organisation shall explore possibilities of shared royalty provisions.

6.4.4 Volunteers and Interns shall be asked to assign their IPR to the organisation using the appropriate agreements in any Works they produce for the organisation. In certain circumstances where this is not appropriate, they shall grant a licence to the organisation to enable reuse of their IPR for all the organisation's purposes.

6.4.5 By arrangement with third parties such as the relevant educational establishment and on a case-by-case basis, as a minimum, the organisation shall ensure that it has a licence to reuse Works produced by students engaged in projects agreed with the educational establishment for all its purposes.

6.5 Unauthorised use of Works

6.5.1 The organisation is committed to respecting Third-party Rights. It is also committed to ensuring that it pursues infringements of the organisation's IPR, where appropriate, so that it can fully use and exploit its own assets and safeguard its collections.

6.5.2 The organisation shall ensure that specific procedures are in place and publicised relating to the alleged infringement of Third-party Rights, in order that any alleged infringements are acknowledged, properly investigated and appropriately followed up.

6.5.3 The organisation shall ensure that procedures are in place and publicised relating to any alleged infringement of the organisation's IPR including where such an infringement causes the organisation to be brought into disrepute.

6.6 Management of IPR

6.6.1 The organisation shall ensure that it manages IPR appropriately in accordance with the principles outlined within this Policy.

6.6.2 The organisation shall put in place the necessary measures to support the principles outlined within this Policy. This shall include a Directorial champion for IPR and regular meetings of a Copyright Working Group to discuss IPR issues across the organisation.

7. Staff training and awareness

7.1 General procedures for the use of Works in accordance with IPR obligations are available from the IP Officer and via the Intranet.

7.2 All staff are required to attend mandatory IP training. Further training will be provided appropriate to the individual's role.

7.3 Staff found to be in breach of this policy will be subject to disciplinary action.

8. General

8.1 This policy is owned by _____ and it was approved on [date].

Appendix 3
Sample data protection policy[1]

Definitions

Data Any information, which is being processed automatically or recorded as part of a relevant, filing system.

Data Controller A person or organisation who (either alone or jointly or in common with other persons) determines the purposes for which and the manner in which any personal data is, or is to be, processed.

Data Subject An individual who is the subject of personal data.

Information Asset Owner The member of staff responsible for collecting the information and/or in charge of the project and/or initiative involving personal data.

Personal Data/Information Data which relates to an identifiable living individual.

Processing Obtaining, accessing, altering, adding to, deleting, changing, disclosing or merging data and anything else, which can be done with data.

Special Category Data Information about an individual's racial or ethnic origin, political opinions, religious beliefs, trade union membership, physical or mental health or condition, sexual life, commission or alleged commission of any offence, any proceedings for any offence committed or alleged to have been committed by him/her.

1. Introduction and scope

1.1 The organisation may collect and hold personal data about its staff, users, visitors, customers, supporters, business partners and other individuals who visit, work with or contact the organisation. It is

---

1. Based on a template created by Naomi Korn Associates.

committed to ensuring that this personal information is managed responsibly and in accordance with data protection legislation, other related policies and any associated legislation or Codes of Practice.

1.2 This policy covers all personal information held by the organisation including that contained in its own records and that held in its archives and deposited collections.

1.3 All the organisation's staff, volunteers and contractors are required to ensure that they comply fully with this policy and its associated procedures.

1.4 This policy is linked closely to the organisation's Acceptable Use Policy. A full list of associated policies can be found in the Appendix.

2. The legislation

2.1 The data protection legislation, namely the Data Protection Act 2018 and the General Data Protection Regulation (GDPR), provides a framework for the handling of Personal Data as well as Special Category Data.

2.2 The data protection legislation applies to all Personal Data and Special Category Data contained in manual files and filing systems, e-mails, computer files, computer databases, images and films, documents and all other formats and media.

2.3 The data protection legislation establishes a number of rights for individuals who are the subjects of such personal data ('Data Subjects') and outlines a number of rights and obligations to those individuals and organisations collecting and using personal data which the organisation must comply with.

3. The role of the Data Protection Officer

3.1 The organisation will ensure it has a Data Protection Officer, who will take responsibility for all matters relating to data protection. The Data Protection Officer for the organisation is _____ .

3.2 The Data Protection Officer shall:
  ◆ inform and advise the organisation about obligations to comply with data protection laws
  ◆ monitor compliance with the Data Protection Act 2018 and GDPR

◆   have appropriate expertise or experience
◆   be the primary Data Protection contact point in the organisation
◆   keep the Privacy Statement current
◆   advise on and monitor Data Protection Impact Assessments
◆   co-operate with the Information Commissioner's Office (ICO) and be the first point of contact
◆   carry out other tasks and duties, provided there is no conflict of interest; so the DPO may hold the asset register and records of the organisation as the central point for ensuring that the organisation is compliant
◆   understand and advise on a risk-based approach to data processing in their organisation.

4. Responsibilities

4.1 _____ , who is the Data Controller, shall take overall responsibility for the organisation's compliance with the Act.

4.2 The technical security of personal data is the responsibility of the _____ , who may, with the agreement of the Data Protection Officer, introduce technical security requirements additional to those outlined in this policy as and when necessary.

4.3 Directors, Assistant Directors and Heads of Department are responsible for the quality, security and management of Personal Data and Special Category Data held by their particular areas. They are responsible for ensuring that this policy is communicated and implemented within their area of responsibility.

4.4 Heads of Department are responsible for large amounts of Personal Data and Special Category Data and take the role of Information Asset Owner. They must register this information with the Data Protection Officer as an Information Asset.

5. Processing Personal Data

5.1 The collection of new categories of Personal Data and/or Special Category Data must be approved by the Head of Department concerned and the Data Protection Officer and only as much should be collected as required.

5.2 When personal information is collected about data subjects, a clear explanation must be provided about how the data will be used. This may be verbally, via a sign (usually in the case of CCTV) or via a statement on a form. All forms requesting personal data, whether electronic or in paper format, will contain a Data Protection Statement, outlining who will use the data and what it will be used for, unless this is already perfectly clear elsewhere on the form. Forms must be approved by the Data Protection Officer before being printed or published on the organisation's website.

5.3 All Personal Data and Special Category Data collected by the organisation or by other organisations on the organisation's behalf, must be collected in accordance with the organisation's Privacy Policy. A link to the Privacy Policy must be available on all web pages where personal data is collected. For personal data collected in other formats the Privacy Policy must be supplied in the most appropriate way.

5.4 The organisation will provide new members of staff with details of how their Personal Data and Special Category Data will be obtained, processed, disclosed and retained.

5.5 Personal Data and Special Category Data must always be collected securely. Web pages collecting personal data shall always be encrypted.

6. Data Subject rights

6.1 Data subjects have the following rights:
- right to be informed
- right of access
- right to rectification
- right to erasure
- right to restrict processing
- right to data portability
- right to object
- rights related to automated decision making.

6.2 The organisation will make available the following information when requested, subject to verification of the enquirer's identity:
- whether the organisation holds any personal data relating to the enquirer and what it is
- why it is held and for what purpose

- how long it will be held for
- who it may be disclosed to
- the logic involved in any automated personal data processing
- their rights concerning that data.

6.3 All requests must be made in writing to the Data Protection Officer. The organisation will comply with written requests within one calendar month of receipt.

7. Using data

7.1 Any access to Personal Data and Special Category Data, including personnel files, marketing databases and CCTV will be encrypted and access limited to authorised personnel only.

7.2 Personal Data and Special Category Data will be kept accurate and up to date and not be held for longer than is necessary, unless it is required for archiving purposes. Personal Data and Special Category Data will have a clear retention period. The organisation's retention schedule, contained within its Record of Processing Activity (ROPA) provides further details of how long certain categories of record should be kept.

7.3 The organisation will only use Personal Data and Special Category Data for the purpose for which it was collected. It will not reuse the data for any other purpose unless the consent is obtained, or if the reuse is allowed by the data protection legislation and approved by the Data Protection Officer.

8. Marketing and sharing data with third parties

8.1 Data subjects will be removed immediately from mailing lists on receipt of a written request.

8.2 Personal Data and Special Category Data will not be shared and/or sold to any outside organisation for use in direct marketing campaigns. Data may be exchanged with similar organisations for use in direct marketing only where the positive consent of the Data Subject and the permission of the Data Protection Officer have been obtained first.

8.3 Personal Data can only be released to external enquirers or shared with other organisations with the prior approval of the Data

Protection Officer and in compliance with the legislation. Occasionally, there will be a legal requirement for the organisation to release information to external organisations; where this is the case, applications should normally be in writing (unless the need is urgent), and be submitted to the Data Protection Officer.

8.4 All requests from third parties to view personal data held by the organisation must be in writing and submitted to the organisation's Data Protection Officer.

8.5 From time to time, the organisation may act as a joint Data Controller for Personal Data collected in partnership with allied organisations for a common purpose. In these cases, the collection, use and management of the data will be subject to a data sharing agreement, signed by a senior manager and approved by the Data Protection Officer.

9. Data breaches

9.1 Personal Data and Special Category Data will be stored securely and in accordance with the organisation's Information Security Policy, Acceptable Use Policy and procedures.

9.2 Staff are responsible for ensuring that Personal Data and Special Category Data is kept securely and is not disclosed, either orally or in writing, to any third party without the permission of the Data Protection Officer.

9.3 All data breaches must be reported immediately to the Data Protection Officer. Breaches must be managed in accordance with the organisation's Data Breach guidance. Serious data breaches shall be reported to the Information Commissioner within 72 hours.

9.4 Personal Data and Special Category Data must be disposed of confidentially and securely, including both digital and print, regardless of format or media.

10. Procurement

10.1 The Data Protection Officer must approve any procurement plans for the management of personal data. This includes the purchase of new IT systems or the outsourcing of the organisation functions where personal data is involved.

10.2 Business cases for new systems or outsourcing the management of personal data must include a Privacy Impact Assessment and specify the requirements for security controls. They must comply with the organisation's Information Security and Management policies.

10.3 Any third party processing personal data on behalf of the organisation will be required to comply with the law and this policy. All outsourcing arrangements must be governed by a contract, which must contain the organisation's standard Data Protection clauses, including a minimum requirement that any data breaches are alerted to the organisation immediately and no longer than 24 hours after discovery. The Data Protection Officer must approve the final contract.

10.4 Personal data is not to be stored or sent outside the European Economic Area (EEA) unless specific safeguards are in place, such as the inclusion of the EU Data Protection clauses in the contract. Special Category Data must always be stored in the EEA.

11. Staff training and awareness

11.1 General procedures for the collection, management and disposal of personal data are available to all staff from the Data Protection Officer and via the Intranet.

11.2 All staff are required to attend mandatory data protection training. Further training will be provided appropriate to the individual's role.

11.3 Staff found to be in breach of this policy will be subject to disciplinary action.

12. General

12.1 This policy is owned by _____ and it was approved on [date].

Appendix 4
Possible contractual terms for online access to database service[1]

This set of clauses assumes a service that is being provided to a private-sector organisation. Services provided to educational establishments, public libraries or archives will require different clauses. Any readers who work in further or higher education are strongly recommended to read the text of the various Jisc model licences,[2] as we consider them to be very fair. Readers who work in public libraries should have a look at the public library licence developed by Licensing Models.[3] Readers who work in the private sector should also check these academic and public library licences for wording that might be useful when negotiating with a database service provider. The clauses below should not be regarded as a 'model contract', but they are presented to give readers an idea of the sorts of clauses that they are likely to encounter. As has been stressed throughout this book, any draft agreement should be negotiated, and explanations sought for the reasons for particular clauses if they are unclear or thought to be unfair.

1. Definitions
In this Agreement, , the following meanings shall apply:

'Provider':	[*name and address*]
'You (and Your)':	the customer identified in the Registration Form, with whom Provider enters into the Agreement,

1. These clauses are based in part upon those provided in Owen, L. (2018) *Clarke's Publishing Agreements: a book of precedents*, Bloomsbury Press. This book explicitly grants permission to purchasers to download the precedents. The clauses provided in *Clarke's Publishing Agreements* upon which this Appendix is based have, however, been amended where appropriate to reflect the views of the authors of this book.
2. See www.jisc-collections.ac.uk/Support/How-Model-Licences-work.
3. www.licensingmodels.com/PublicLibrariesLicense

	and any person who Provider reasonably believes is acting with the customer's authority
'Account':	the facility extended under this Agreement allowing You to access and use the Service
'Agreement':	the entire contract between Provider and You for the provision of the Service incorporating these terms and conditions, the Registration Form, and the documents referred to in them
'Approved Use':	your private and internal business use only
'Authorised Users':	the users notified to Provider in the Registration Form
'Data':	the information and other materials in whatever form from time to time available through the Service
'Fees':	the charges for the Service as set out and amended from time to time in the Provider's price list
'Passwords':	unique user names and codes
'Registration Form':	the Service registration form
'Rights':	copyright, database and other intellectual property and related rights owned by the Provider and its licensors
'Service':	[*insert name of service*]
'Start Date':	[*date*]
'Term':	[*period*]

2. Registration

2.1 In order to register for the Service and set up Your Account You must complete the Registration Form. You confirm that all the details supplied by You when You register are accurate and complete. You agree to notify the Service help desk promptly of any changes. The Agreement shall not be binding until Provider has issued its acceptance to You.

2.2 The details You provide to Provider will be used to provide the Service to You. Your details including those of your Authorised Users will not be supplied to any third parties except with your explicit written consent, or where required by law. Please contact the Service help desk to withdraw those consents at any time.

2.3 In order to operate Your Account You will be issued with one or more Passwords. You are responsible for the security and proper use of Your Passwords and Your Account, including all charges incurred through them. You must inform the Service help desk immediately if You have any reason to believe that Your Passwords have become known to someone not authorised to use them. If Provider reasonably believes that there is likely to be a breach of security or misuse of the Service or Your Account, it may change Your Passwords immediately and will notify You accordingly.

3. Provision of the Service

3.1 Provider will provide the Service and Your Account in accordance with the terms and conditions of the Agreement.

3.2 The Service is accessed via the internet. You are responsible for all costs necessary to enable You to access the Service and receive the Data. Contact the Service help desk for further details of minimum technical requirements. Provider will not be able to issue refunds or accept responsibility for any delay or inability to access any part of the Service or the Data due to any faults of, or Your means of access to, the internet.[4]

3.3 Provider cannot guarantee that the Service will never be faulty or that it will be available at all times but Provider will endeavour to correct reported faults as soon as Provider reasonably can. If a fault occurs You should report the fault to the Service help desk. Provider may need to vary the technical specification, or temporarily suspend the whole or any part, of the Service from time to time but shall give You as much notice as is reasonably practicable in the circumstances.

4. Use of the Data

4.1 The Service enables You to download Data. Provider grants You a non-exclusive, non-transferable licence to use the Data on the following terms. Unless indicated to the contrary on the Service, any

---

4. The client may well wish to include minimum service requirements, such as maximum permitted down time, here.

Data You download may be viewed on screen and printed out in hard copy for Approved Use.

4.2 You must not, nor attempt to, resell, make available on a wide area network or distribute externally the Service or the Data (in whole or in part) to any third party. Any Data that You download must be held securely within Your possession, free from any third-party access and with all credits, legends, notices or markings maintained. [*Make clear whether distribution on a LAN, linking to, including in an archival or searchable database, is permitted or not. Make clear whether remote access is permitted or not.*]

4.3 You may make such temporary electronic copies of the Data as is reasonably necessary to enable the Approved Use. Provider and its licensors reserve all other Rights.

4.4 Provider warrants that Your use of the Data in accordance with the terms of this Agreement shall not infringe the Rights of any third party. You must contact Provider immediately if anyone makes or threatens to make a claim against You relating to Your use of the Data and You will comply with any reasonable request from Provider in relation to such claim.

5. Charges

5.1 You must pay the Fees due for the access and use of the Service and the Data through Your Account in accordance with this clause.

5.2 You will be invoiced [*frequency*] in arrears for the Fees due. Each invoice will be payable within 30 days of the date stated on the invoice. If You do not pay an invoice in cleared funds within that period, Provider may: (i) charge interest on any outstanding moneys due at a rate of [__] per cent (__%) above the [__] plc base rate from time to time in force calculated on a daily basis; and/or (ii) suspend Your Passwords and Your Account, until payment in full is made.

5.3 On expiration or termination of this Agreement for whatever reason: (i) Provider shall terminate Your access to the Service; (ii) You and Your Authorised Users shall have no further right to access or use the Data; [*and (iii) You must permanently delete or otherwise destroy any copies of the Data in Your possession or control.*]

5.4 All Fees are quoted exclusive of any applicable value added tax which shall be payable by You.

6. Term and termination

6.1 The Agreement shall commence on the Start Date and continue for the Term unless terminated earlier in accordance with the following provisions.

6.2 In addition to any other rights either party may have, either party can terminate the Agreement immediately without notice if the other party: (i) breaches any provision of this Agreement and fails to remedy that breach within seven working days upon notice; or (ii) is made bankrupt, enters into liquidation or any arrangement or composition with its creditors or if a receiver or administrator or administrative receiver is appointed against any of its assets or business or if it suffers any analogous event in any jurisdiction.

6.3 If either party delays in acting upon a breach of this Agreement by the other party, that delay will not be regarded as a waiver of the breach.

7. Liability

7.1 Whilst Provider will use all reasonable skill and care in the creation and supply of the Service and the Data, Provider does not give any warranty as to its suitability, accuracy or fitness for any purpose.

7.2 Subject to Clauses 7.3 and 7.4, Provider excludes all liability whether in contract, tort (including liability for negligence) or otherwise for the suitability, accuracy or fitness for any purpose of the Service and any Data and limits its liability for any other liability under this Agreement to the Fees payable by You for the element of the Service or the Data in dispute.

7.3 Subject to Clause 7.4, Provider excludes all liability for loss of business revenue or profits, anticipated savings or wasted expenditure, corruption or destruction of data and for any indirect or consequential loss whatsoever.

7.4 Provider does not limit or exclude its liability for death or personal injury caused by its negligence or any other liability the limitation or exclusion of which is prohibited by law.

7.5 All warranties, conditions or other terms implied by statute or common law are only excluded to the extent permitted by law.

8. General

8.1 You agree to keep confidential (both during and after the Term) the contents of the Agreement. This does not apply to any disclosure required by a court or regulatory body of competent jurisdiction, trivial information or information already publicly available or demonstrably in Your possession at the time of disclosure (other than as a result of breach of any confidentiality obligation).

8.2 Provider may modify the Agreement at any time, such modifications becoming effective immediately upon either posting of the modified Agreement on the Service or notification to You. All Data advertised on the Service may be amended or replaced without notice at any time. Following any modification of the Service or the Data contained in the Service, You may cancel this Agreement by giving the Provider [*time period*] written notice of such cancellation. If You do cancel, You must pay any remaining charges due to Provider.

8.3 You are not allowed to transfer or attempt to transfer this Agreement in whole or in part to a third party without Provider's express written permission.

8.4 Neither party will be liable if it cannot perform its obligation under this Agreement because of circumstances beyond its reasonable control such as technical failure, severe weather, fire or explosion, civil disorder, war, or military operations, natural or local emergency, anything done by government or other competent authority or industrial disputes of any kind.

8.5 Notices given under the Agreement may be given by one party to the other either online through the Service or in writing to the address as currently stated in this Agreement.

8.6 The provisions of this Agreement are without limitation to the rights of You or Authorised Users to do any act permitted under the Copyright, Design and Patents Act 1988, including Chapter III (*Acts Permitted in relation to Copyright Works*) or any supervening legislation, or permitted under any CC-BY or other open access licence applicable to the Data which, apart from the rights granted under this Agreement would not infringe the intellectual property rights in the Data and, notwithstanding any provision of this Agreement, You and Authorised Users shall remain entitled to do any such acts.

8.7 This Agreement is the entire and only agreement between the parties concerning its subject matter and supersedes all prior agreements, arrangements and understandings (whether written or oral) relating thereto. Nothing in this Agreement shall limit or exclude either party's liability for fraud.

8.8 This Agreement is governed by, and construed in accordance with, English law and You and Provider submit to the non-exclusive jurisdiction of the English courts as regards any claim or matter arising in relation to this Agreement.

Appendix 5
Data protection privacy notice template[1]

Many such templates are also available online. We recommend that readers consult the ICO's website aimed at small-to-medium-size enterprises.[2] The web page includes background information to GDPR, together with a suggested template privacy notice, which can be downloaded and then amended to suit a particular organisation's requirements.

Privacy Notices, often called Privacy Policies or Statements, must be used by every organisation and written in clear and plain language. They should be concise, and easily accessible. The purpose of a Privacy Notice is to inform a data subject of his/her rights regarding the processing of his/her data. Privacy notices may be displayed in many different places, for example, in forms, in contracts, websites, or on notice boards. It is an externally facing explanation of how you manage personal data responsibly and with respect.

If personal data is being provided by a data subject, your privacy notice or a link to it should be provided at the time that the data is collected. Here are some useful links:

◆ See https://ico.org.uk/for-organisations/guide-to-the-general-data-protection-regulation-gdpr for general guidance.
◆ Department or Education model privacy notice: www.gov.uk/government/publications/data-protection-and-privacy-privacy-notices.
◆ Also see www.nationalarchives.gov.uk/information-management/legislation/data-protection for guidance on archiving personal data.

---

1. Based on a template developed by Naomi Korn Associates.
2. See https://ico.org.uk/for-organisations/business

Your obligations regarding accessibility to information in the Privacy Notice

When should the policy about the use of personal data be provided to data subjects?	If the personal data is collected directly by a Data Controller: When the data is obtained	If personal data is received by the data controller from a third party: 1 within 1 month of receiving the data 2 when first contact is made with the data subject 3 if further disclosure of the data to a third party is envisaged, before that data.

What you should include in your Privacy Notice

What information should a Privacy Notice contain to inform the Data Subject?	Personal Data collected by Data Controller from a Data Subject	Personal Data received by Data Controller from a Third Party
Introduction setting out the importance of protecting personal data to your organisation		
Identify your organisation as Data Controller and/or Data Processor and your contact details		
Contact details of the Data Protection Officer or data protection lead as appropriate		
What data you are collecting. The type, or category of personal data e.g. names, addresses, passwords, bank details Does the data come from publicly accessible sources?		

What information should a Privacy Notice contain to inform the Data Subject?	Personal Data collected by Data Controller from a Data Subject	Personal Data received by Data Controller from a Third Party
What you do with the data and how it is used, i.e. the purpose of the processing.		
The lawful basis for processing. Drawn from the six options e.g. consent, contract, legitimate interest, etc. Set out which bases you are relying upon.		
Where the data is stored and the data security arrangements you have in place. Information about any transfers beyond the EEA.		
How long you hold the information. Retention schedules or spreadsheets showing the different periods and/or criteria used to decide on retention periods.		
The rights to control their personal data: ◆ right to be informed ◆ right of access ◆ right to correct inaccurate data ◆ right to delete information ◆ right to object to processing ◆ right to data portability ◆ right to withdraw consent ◆ right to restrict processing		

What information should a Privacy Notice contain to inform the Data Subject?	Personal Data collected by Data Controller from a Data Subject	Personal Data received by Data Controller from a Third Party
Where the provision of personal data is part of a contractual/statutory requirement explain the possible consequences of not providing the personal data.		
Where automated decision making in the processing of data is being undertaken.		
The use of cookies on websites. Where more detail is required link to the Cookies Policy.		
Use of links to third party websites from your website and the need for care.		
Options to complain to the Information Commissioner's Office if you are unable to resolve matters, with contact details.		
The regular review of this Privacy Notice.		

Disclaimer: None of the information contained within this document should be construed as legal advice. Should specific legal advice be required, please consult the appropriate legal advisor.

Bibliography

Boren, J. (2016) *For Intellectual Property*, self-published.

Brown, A. (ed.) (2019) *Intellectual Property, Climate Change and Technology: managing national legal intersections, relationships and conflicts*, Edward Elgar.

Burk, Jr, C. F. and Horton, F. W. (1988) *InfoMap: a complete guide to discovering corporate information resources*, Prentice-Hall.

Cabinet Office (2018) *Freedom of Information Code of Practice*, https://assets.publishing.service.gov.uk/government/uploads/system/ uploads/attachment_data/file/744071/CoP_FOI_Code_of_Practice_- _Minor_Amendments_20180926_.pdf.

Callaghan, S. (2017) Has the Introduction of Orphan Works Licensing Schemes Solved the Problem that Orphan Works Present to Digitization Projects?, *Archives and Records*, **38** (2), 244–56.

Carey, P. (2018) *Data Protection: a practical guide to UK and EU law*, 5th edn, OUP.

Cavoukian, A. (2011) *Privacy by Design: the 7 foundational principles*, www.ipc.on.ca/wpcontent/uploads/Resources/ 7foundationalprinciples.pdf.

Chapdelaine, P. (2017) *Copyright User Rights: contracts and the erosion of property*, OUP.

Copyright Act 1911.

Copyright Act 1956.

Copyright, Designs and Patents Act 1988.

Copyright and Related Rights Regulations 2003, SI 2003/2498.

Copyright and Rights in Performances (Research, Education, Libraries and Archives) Regulations 2014, 2014/1372.

Copyright and Rights in Performances (Certain Permitted Uses of Orphan Works) Regulations 2014, S.I. 2014/2861.

Cornish, G. P. (2019). *Copyright*, 6th edn rev., Facet Publishing.

Council Directive (EC) 2012/28/EU on certain permitted uses of orphan works Text with EEA relevance. [2012] OJ L299.

Council Directive (EC) 2019/790 on copyright and related rights in the Digital Single Market and amending Directives 96/9/EC and 2001/29/EC. [2019] OJ L130.

Council Regulation (EC) 2016/679 on the protection of natural persons with regard to the processing of personal data and on the free movement of such data, and repealing Directive 95/46/EC (General Data Protection Regulation).

Data Protection Act 1984.

Data Protection Act 1998.

Data Protection Act 2018, www.legislation.gov.uk/ukpga/2018/12/contents/enacted.

Denley, A., Foulsham, M. and Hitchen, B. (2019) *GDPR: how to achieve and maintain compliance*, Routledge.

Directive (EC) 2003/4 on public access to environmental information and repealing Council Directive 90/313/EEC OJ L41.

Directive (EC) 2003/98 on the re-use of public sector information OJ L345.

Directive (EC) 2012/28/EU on certain permitted uses of orphan works. OJ L299.

Durrant, F. (2006) *Negotiating Licences for Digital Resources*, Facet Publishing.

Eblida (2015) *Fair Copyright for All Across Europe: rallying call from libraries, archives and charities*, www.eblida.org/news/fair-copyright-for-all-across-europe.html.

Fine, J. (2017) Negotiating with Ghosts: the arbitrariness of copyright terms, *Intellectual Property Journal (Canada)*, **29** (2), 333–54.

Freedom of Information Act 2000.

Freedom of Information (Scotland) Act 2002, asp 13.

Freedom of Information (Release of Datasets for Re-use) (Fees) Regulations 2013, SI 2003/1977.

Gibbons, P. (2019) *The Freedom of Information Officer's Handbook*, Facet Publishing.

Harris, L. E. (2018) *Licensing Digital Content*, 3rd edn, American Library Association.

Hawley, R. (1995) *Information as an Asset: the board agenda*, KPMG Impact Programme.

Holtz, L. E., Nocun, K. and Hansen, M. (2011) Towards Displaying

Privacy Information with Icons. In Fischer-Hu et al. (eds) *Privacy and Identity 2010 (Advances in Information and Communication Technology 352)*, Springer, 338–48.

Information Commissioner's Office (2014) *The Right to Recorded Information and Requests for Documents*, https://ico.org.uk/media/for-organisations/documents/1621/the-right-to-recorded-information-and-requests-for-documents.pdf.

Information Commissioner's Office (2015) *Datasets (sections 11, 19 & 45) Freedom of Information Act*, https://ico.org.uk/media/for-organisations/documents/1151/datasets-foi-guidance.pdf.

Information Commissioner's Office (2016) *Section 46 Code of Practice – Records Management*, https://ico.org.uk/media/for-organisations/documents/1624142/section-46-code-of-practice-records-management-foia-and-eir.pdf.

Information Commissioner's Office (2019) *Data Protection Officers*, https://ico.org.uk/for-organisations/guide-to-data-protection/guide-to-the-general-data-protection-regulation-gdpr/accountability-and-governance/data-protection-officers.

Intellectual Property Office (2014) Explanatory Memorandum to The Copyright and Rights in Performances (Research, Education, Libraries and Archives) Regulations 2014 2014 no. 1372, The Copyright and Rights in Performances (Disability) Regulations 2014 2014 no. 1384 and The Copyright (Public Administration) Regulations 2014 2014 no. 1385, www.legislation.gov.uk/uksi/2014/1372/memorandum/contents.

Intellectual Property Office (2015a) *Orphan Works Licensing Scheme Overview for Applicants*, https://assets.publishing.service.gov.uk/government/uploads/system/uploads/attachment_data/file/518251/Orphan_Works_Licensing_Scheme_Overview_for_Applicants.pdf.

Intellectual Property Office (2015b) *Orphan Works: review of the first twelve months*, https://assets.publishing.service.gov.uk/government/uploads/system/uploads/attachment_data/file/487209/orphan-works-annual-report.pdf.

Intellectual Property Office (2018a) *Changes to Copyright Law in the Event of No Deal*, www.gov.uk/government/publications/changes-to-copyright-law-in-the-event-of-no-deal/changes-to-copyright-law-in-the-event-of-no-deal#mutual-recognition-of-orphan-works.

Intellectual Property Office (2018b*) Orphan Works Diligent Search Guidance for Applicants: guidance on searching for right holders in copyright works to obtain permission to reproduce the work,* www.gov.uk/government/publications/changes-to-copyright-law-in-the-event-of-no-deal/changes-to-copyright-law-in-the-event-of-no-deal#mutual-recognition-of-orphan-works.

Jay, R. (2017) *Guide to the General Data Protection Regulation: a companion to Data Protection Law and Practice (4th edition),* Sweet & Maxwell.

Jones, H. and Benson, C. (2016) *Publishing Law,* 5th edn, Routledge.

Kinsella, S. (2015) *Against Intellectual Property,* Mises Institute.

Martin, B. (1998) *Information Liberation,* Freedom Press.

Martinez, M. and Terras, M. (2019) 'Not Adopted': the UK Orphan Works Licensing Scheme and how the crisis of copyright in the cultural heritage sector restricts access to digital content, *Open Library of Humanities,* **5** (1): 36, 1–51.

Mehldau, M. (2007) Iconset for Data-Privacy Declarations v0.1, http://netzpolitik.org/wp-upload/data-privacy-icons-v01.pdf.

Michaels, A. and Norris, A. (2014) *A Practical Guide to Trade Mark Law,* 5th edn, OUP.

Oppenheim, C., Stenson, J. and Wilson, R. M. S. (2002) The Attributes of Information as an Asset, Its Measurement and Role in Enhancing Organisational Effectiveness. In Stein, J., Kyrillidou, M., and Davis, D. (eds) *Proceedings of the 4th Northumbria International Conference on Performance Measurement in Libraries and Information Services 'Meaningful Measures for Emerging Realities', Sheraton Station Square Conference Center, Pittsburgh, Pennsylvania, 12 to 16 August 2001,* Association of Research Libraries, 197–201.

Owen, L. (2018) *Clark's Publishing Agreements: a book of precedents,* 10th edn, Bloomsbury.

Padfield, T. (2019) *Copyright for Archivists and Records Managers,* 6th edn, Facet Publishing.

Public Records Act 1958.

Regulation (EC) No 1049/2001 regarding public access to European Parliament, Council and Commission documents OJ L145.

Regulation (EC) on the protection of natural persons with regard to the processing of personal data on the free movement of such data, and repealing Directive 95/46/EC (Data Protection Directive).

Stobo, V., Patterson, K. and Deazley, R. (2017) *Digitisation and Risk*, www.digitisingmorgan.org/Risk.

Stobo, V., Erickson, K., Bertoni, A. and Guerrieri, F. (2018) *Current Best Practices Among Cultural Heritage Institutions When Dealing With Copyright Orphan Works and Analysis of Crowdsourcing Options*, http://diligentsearch.eu/wp-content/uploads/2018/05/EnDOW-Report-3.pdf.

The Environmental Information Regulations 2004, SI 2004/3391.

The Environmental Information (Scotland) Regulations 2004, SSI 2004/520).

The Privacy and Electronic Communications (EC Directive) Regulations 2003, SI 2003/2426.

The Re-use of Public Sector Information Regulations 2015, SI 2015/1415.

Voigt, P. and von dem Bussche, A. (2017) *The EU GDPR: a practical guide*, Springer.

Williams, A., Calow, D. and Lee, A. (2011) *Digital Media Contracts*, Oxford University Press.

Willinsky, J. (2018) *The Intellectual Properties of Learning*, University of Chicago Press.

Index

Note: The index covers the Introduction and the numbered chapters but not the Appendices. An *italic* page reference indicates that relevant information can be found in a Figure on that page; **bold** references are to tables while the letter 'n' refers to a numbered footnote.

The authors would like to thank Bill Johncocks, who prepared this index.